1 Alexandra Palace

ISLINGTON

KING'S CROSS

HOXTON

PENTONVILLE ▶ 83
Pentonville Road   City Road

ST PANCRAS

CLERKENWELL

SHOREDITCH

BLOOMSBURY
11

5

HOLBORN

SOHO

WHITECHAPEL

2

6
ST JAMES'S
3
41

SOUTHWARK

THE BOROUGH

Westminster Bridge Road   Borough Road

Long Lane

1

BERMONDSEY

WESTMINSTER

NEWINGTON

7

3 →
Greenwich Market

LAMBETH

8 Rosebery's

2 Ardingly
45 miles/ 72 km

The London
Antiques
Guide

Kimberly Jayne Gray

The London
Antiques
Guide

Street-by-Street ▪ Style-by-Style

With 197 color illustrations and 11 maps

 Thames & Hudson

For updates see *www.london-antiques-guide.com*

Layout © 2005 Thames & Hudson Ltd, London
Text and photographs © 2005 Kimberly Jayne Gray (*www.londonside.com*)
Photo on back flap © 2005 Peter Finlay

First published in 2005 in paperback in the United States of America by
Thames & Hudson Inc., 500 Fifth Avenue, New York, New York 10110

thamesandhudsonusa.com

Library of Congress Catalog Card Number 2004112480

ISBN 13: 978-0-500-28540-4

ISBN 10: 0-500-28540-3

Printed and bound in China by Midas Printing Ltd

Contents

Introduction

FOREWORD BY MICHAEL LIPITCH

As a dealer and professional tour guide, Kimberly is your ideal escort around London – one of the world's richest sources of antiques. Finding dealers and other venues with consistently interesting and high-quality items in this thriving metropolis can be a challenge. This refreshingly accessible, wonderfully functional and superbly illustrated guide pinpoints the very essence of sourcing antiques: knowing where to go for those great buys.

I first met Kimberly a number of years ago when she agreed to help me during the week of Grosvenor House Art and Antiques Fair, although she actually ended up staying for three years. She has had to learn this trade the hard way! In my own career, one of my greatest tools has been a well-worn map of Britain, marked with the locations of hundreds of fantastic dealers. Some I came across on my travels, but many sources were passed down to me by my father and grandfather, who were also in the antiques field. These tips have proved invaluable.

The London Antiques Guide offers an insider's perspective on many such gems, with over 350 of London's essential antiques sources, and many of its best-kept secrets. Gone are the days of trudging to shops only to find disappointing stock or unexpected high prices – or worse still, that they are closed when you arrive. Many of the trade's hotspots – such as **King's Road** and **Fulham Road**, or **Kensington Church Street** and **Portobello Road** – stand side by side, making it easy to browse what's on offer before parting with any of your hard-earned cash. The extensive list of websites woven into the text will enable you to expand your search from the comfort of your own home.

This truly fantastic guide will benefit the traditional antiquarian, the collector, the designer, the enthusiast and the novice alike. By doing all the strenuous work for you, Kimberly allows you to concentrate on developing your eye and taste so that you can relish the really enjoyable experience of antiques – finding a wonderful piece and buying it.

How to Use this Guide

There are seven accessible sections within this book, designed to help you survey London's antiques quarters by area and style. They contain information on all types of venue – from shops and auction houses to fairs and markets. A full glossary of general trade terms and phrases appears at the end of the book along with a quick price guide, two timelines and various tips and tricks of the trade.

Street-by-Street highlights London's antiques hotspots, ordered in a logical sequence by location. This format will enable you to travel easily from one street to the next or to concentrate on one particular area. Headings for auction houses, fairs, markets and styles have been listed alphabetically for easy reference, although areas and outlets featured within these sections follow the same location-based format as Street-by-Street.

Names of the streets and styles listed individually (for instance **Fulham Road** or **Art Nouveau**) are cross-referenced in **bold** type when mentioned in passing and are also colour-coded by section. The symbol ▶ signifies that full details of that shop or outlet have already been given, and the following number refers you to the relevant page.

London Essentials

Maps: This guide features eleven maps in total, which all follow a simple, easy-to-use format. The general map inside the jacket of this book is designed to give you an overview of London and the relative locations of all the areas, which are often clustered together – for instance **King's Road** and **Fulham Road**, which are just a few streets apart. There is a key to the left of the map for quick reference. There are also ten more detailed maps within the book (one for each of the areas in Street-by-Street), which pinpoint key roads and any tube stations in the vicinity.

Transport: Log on to Transport for London's (TFL) website at *http://tube.tfl.gov.uk* for comprehensive information on both tube and bus services, including maps and timetables. The TUBE is the most practical and often the fastest way to travel, particularly if you are not familiar with London. Tickets are priced according to zone, and it is always cheaper to buy a daily or weekly travelcard if you are planning to shop around. There are six zones in total (with Zone One covering central London), but all of the streets in the Street-by-Street section are in either Zone One or Two. A few of the shops featured in chapters 2–7 lie beyond Zone Two, so make sure you check before you get your ticket. There are clear price listings in each tube station (generally by the ticket machines), which are ordered alphabetically by destination, as well as maps and other useful information. Although operating times vary from line to line, in general the tube runs from 5.30 a.m. until midnight.

Those of you who are fascinated by London's rich history should keep an eye out for the city's forty-odd ghost stations, which are scattered along the tracks. Some of these abandoned stations have disappeared, but there are a few noteworthy exceptions. For instance, there used to be a station between Tottenham Court Road and Holborn on the Central line. It was closed in 1933, but you can still see the remains of its white-tiled walls from the train. Further information is available on TFL's website.

You could also try out London's famous double decker BUSES, which can be slow but are comparatively cheap. You can buy a ticket on most bus routes, although some do require you to buy your ticket before you board. These routes are clearly marked by a yellow strip on the bus stop sign, and there are roadside machines at all such bus stops. Pre-pay is being introduced increasingly to routes in central London. Remember that children under the age of eleven are allowed to travel free at any time.

If you cannot face public transport and decide to hail a TAXI, make sure you get a registered black cab. Unlicensed vehicles can be costly and unsafe. There are marked taxi ranks at London's mainline stations, but often you will have no trouble flagging down a cab, particularly in central London. This is not an option if you're on a tight budget – depending on your journey, a daily taxi allowance of £40–80 would not be unrealistic.

Driving your own CAR in London is not advisable, however tempting it may seem. The roads are extremely busy, it is very difficult (and expensive) to park, and there is also a congestion charge if you enter central London by car during certain times.

Payment Methods: Many dealers, especially those in the £5,000-and-under price bracket, do not take DEBIT or CREDIT CARDS. Dealers with the facility to take cards often do so only as a last resort due to the fees they incur. Therefore, if you are spending relatively little, CASH is the easiest payment method. For those of you who have travelled to London from abroad, the UK's high-street banks (such as HSBC, Barclays and Natwest) can be found all over London and are usually open from 9.30 a.m. until 4 or 5 p.m. Monday to Friday. Cash machines generally restrict you to a daily withdrawal limit of about £300. There are also plenty of bureaux de change all over the city, particularly at mainline train stations and in central London, which often open much later. Few people use £50 notes, which are often treated with suspicion .

For more costly items, TRAVELLER'S CHEQUES (such as American Express [Amex], Visa and Thomas Cook) can be used, although most dealers will ask that you cash them at a bank or bureau de change. Usually you will be charged one or two per cent, and it is important to retain the purchase agreement and the serial numbers of your cheques, all of which should be kept separate from the cheques themselves.

For expensive purchases, antique shops often prefer you to leave a deposit and wire the outstanding balance across. In this case the dealer will provide you with an invoice with his or her banking details (the bank name, address, account number and sort code). With this information you will be able to send a wire from your bank at home for a cost of about £15 to £20 which should take a few working days to arrive. If you pay by this method, the dealer will probably want to hold the piece until payment has been received. Sometimes the dealer will allow the shipper to collect but ask that the shipper wait to release the shipment until he or she has been paid.

A final way to arrange payment for goods is to set up what is called a BUYER'S ACCOUNT with a shipper. This must be pre-arranged with your shipper and requires you to wire one amount of money which will be held in an account with the shipper. When you purchase a piece from a dealer, you will simply leave a collection note with the dealer, and the shipper will pay on your behalf when he or she collects the piece. This is a practical method if you intend to purchase a large number of goods and ship them out of the country (▶ 145–147) as it requires only one wire transfer. However, be sure to use a reputable shipper whom you trust.

Safety Awareness: Like most cities, pick-pocketing is common in London. It is best to carry valuables under your clothing or in an unobtrusive carrier bag.

1 Street-by-Street

The majority of London's antiques sources are concentrated in and around the streets listed in this chapter. They all have their own particular characteristics and charms, but prices and quality can vary enormously. Each profile sets the scene, with full details on where to go, how to get there, what to see, where to eat, and what to do when you're done with antiques. There are also colour maps for each area.

Decorative

LILLIE ROAD FULHAM

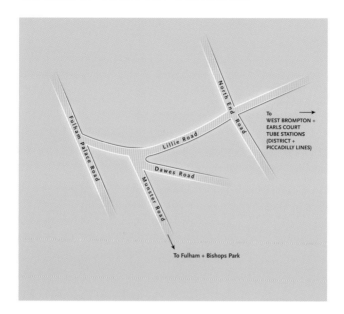

WHAT'S THERE?

Although it was only a country road until the 19th century, today Lillie Road is renowned for decorative antiques. The first antique shops began to spring up in the 1980s as dealers searched for lower rents within a stone's throw of fashionable Kensington, Chelsea and Fulham.

From these few shops, Lillie Road has developed into a considerable force in the world of decorative antiques, and it is a goldmine of pretty and whimsical objects. Expect **shabby chic**, with white **painted French** pieces from the 19th century, as well as more modern, quirky pieces from the 19th and 20th centuries.

Many of the dealers on Lillie Road are young and keen to turn around their stock quickly. They offer charming, comfortable pieces that do not have to cost the earth.

WHEN IS IT OPEN?

Shops are generally open Monday to Saturday from 10 a.m. to 5.30 p.m. Some shops have slightly erratic hours, especially on a Saturday, as often there is only one person to run the shop and buy for the business.

HOW TO GET THERE

The nearest tube station to the Munster Road end of Lillie Road is Parsons Green (District line), although it is quite a walk. As you exit the station, turn left down Parsons

Green Lane, cross over **Fulham Road**, and carry on up Kelvedon Road until you hit Bishops Road. Turn left down Bishops Road until you reach the second crossroads along. Turn right up Munster Road, which leads into Lillie Road. Alternatively, you could go to Earls Court tube station (District and Piccadilly lines) or West Brompton (District line) and catch the 74 bus to the intersection of Lillie Road and Dawes Road.

HIGHLIGHTS

Great finds can be discovered on Lillie Road, and you may pick up a charming piece for as little as £100. The stock is mixed in terms of quality and price, making this street London's treasure-hunt hotspot. It is a great starting point for novice or inexperienced collectors, and the dealers tend to be quite approachable.

LOWLIGHTS

Lillie Road is harder to get to than other antiques districts. Also, you may find objects that are not as old as they seem, as many dealers favour style and decorative potential over purity. If it seems too good to be true in terms of price, date and style, it usually is.

WHERE TO GO

Rainbow 329 LILLIE ROAD, LONDON SW6 7NR
℗ 020 7385 1323 *www.rainbowlondon.com*
Rainbow is a specialist in lighting, with hundreds of Italian late 19th- and early 20th-century chandeliers and sconces from which to choose.

Fulham Antiques 320 MUNSTER ROAD,
LONDON SW6 6BH ℗ 020 7610 3644
On the corner of Munster Road and Lillie Road, Fulham Antiques is packed with traditional brown antiques chosen for their decorative quality.

Curious Science 319 LILLIE ROAD, LONDON SW6 7LL
℗ 020 7610 1175 *www.curiousscience.com*
A science lover's haven, this shop sells all kinds of medical and scientific antiques, including globes, microscopes, and marine and natural history items.

3 one 3 Antiques 313 LILLIE ROAD, LONDON SW6 7LL ℗ 020 7381 2404
Brown furniture is brightened by unusual and decorative chandeliers and ceramics at this traditional antique shop.

Architectural Antiques 312 LILLIE ROAD,
LONDON SW6 7PS ℗ 020 7385 3519
Across the street and below a hairdresser's, this brilliant, small architectural **salvage** shop stocks fireplaces, stone, statues, garden objects and lighting, all with flair and masculine style. With a little imagination you will see boundless possibilities.

301 301 LILLIE ROAD, LONDON SW6 7LL ℗ 020 7385 4999
301 offers traditional brown furniture from the 19th and early 20th centuries as well as ceramics, glass and prints.

297 297 LILLIE ROAD, LONDON SW6 7LL ✆ 020 7386 1888
Here you will find one of the **new school** of antique shops, where the dealers have a real flair for design and presentation. Andrew Harley and Laraine Plummer sell a mixture of antiques ripe with whimsy, irony and flair. Also, be sure to visit the basement for more **rustic** or decorative antiques.

295 295 LILLIE ROAD, LONDON SW6 7LL ✆ 020 7381 5277
A shop with an ever-changing stock, mood and look, on any given day 295 can have French chateau doors, 20th-century design and English 18th-century furniture together with vintage items from the 1970s.

291 Decorative Antiques 291 LILLIE ROAD,
LONDON SW6 7LL ✆ 020 7381 5008
Several dealers pack this shop with a range of traditional and decorative antiques, including furniture, objects and textiles.

Andrew Bewick 287 LILLIE ROAD, LONDON SW6 7LL ✆ 020 7385 9025
This charming shop sells furniture and objects with a pleasing, soft look. Bewick carries a full selection of traditional English and **French painted** pieces as well as **rustic** and distressed items.

Stephen Sprake Antiques 283 LILLIE ROAD,
LONDON SW6 7LL ✆ 020 7381 3209
Stephen Sprake creates a surprising and commanding look with furniture from the 18th century to the 1960s, as well as lighting, metalwork and mirrors. Sprake's fantasia of decorative and eclectic items resonates with irony, placing him firmly in the **new school** of antiques.

Decorative Antiques 284 LILLIE ROAD,
LONDON SW6 7PX ✆ 020 7610 2694
This Lillie Road staple stocks painted, provincial and charming antique furniture and objects for the **shabby chic** and relaxed styles. Inexpensive prices and a popular look make for a high turnover. You never know what you may find – only that it will probably be gone by the time you come again.

Hindley 281 LILLIE ROAD, LONDON SW6 7LL ✆ 020 7385 0706
Traditional antiques from the 19th and early 20th centuries (particularly furniture and mirrors) are the order of the day at Hindley.

Martagon 279 LILLIE ROAD, LONDON SW6 7LL ✆ 020 7385 9050
Several dealers stock Martagon with flair and panache, selling charming, decorative French antiques and smalls together with metalwork. Martagon's stunning look is perfected in the interior design of dealers Jim and Andrew's gorgeous French chateau/hotel near Bordeaux (*www.chateau-st-vincent.com*).

Nimmo & Spooner 277 LILLIE ROAD,
LONDON SW6 7LL ✆ 020 7385 2724
Nimmo & Spooner stocks late 18th- to early 20th-century antique furniture and garden pieces with a relaxed and distressed look.

275 Antiques 275 LILLIE ROAD, LONDON SW6 7LL ☎ 020 7386 7382
With eclectic English and French furniture from the 18th to the 20th century, 275 specializes in 1920s and 30s ceramics, particularly Susie Cooper, and 1970s and 1980s perspex furniture.

Artefact 273 LILLIE ROAD, LONDON SW6 7LL ☎ 020 7381 2500
Victoria adeptly sets the style and standard for Lillie Road with charming antique and vintage pieces that create the ever popular distressed, soft and pale look. Expect chandeliers, aged mirrors and **painted French** furniture, all beautifully displayed.

Graham Kirkland 271 LILLIE ROAD, LONDON SW6 7LL
☎ 020 7381 3195 *www.grahamkirkland.co.uk*
This unusual shop is a must-see for all things ecclesiastical and Gothic.

269 Antiques 269 LILLIE ROAD, LONDON SW6 7LL ☎ 020 7610 1498
At 269 you will find **painted** and gilt **French** 19th- and early 20th-century antiques with a pretty and relaxed look.

WHERE TO EAT

Delitalia 325 LILLIE ROAD, LONDON SW6 7NR ☎ 020 7386 5701
This small, authentic Italian sandwich bar is definitely the best place to stop for either a coffee or delicious ciabatta sandwich in the Lillie Road vicinity. You can also purchase Italian speciality foods in the small deli.

The Chancery 316 LILLIE ROAD, LONDON SW6 7PS ☎ 020 7385 2658
This Victorian pub offers up hot food and sandwiches in gastro pub style. With high ceilings, stained glass and a decidedly laid-back atmosphere, stop at The Chancery for lunch (12–3 p.m.) or a drink while on Lillie Road.

WHILE YOU'RE IN THE AREA

Museum of Fulham Palace BISHOPS AVENUE,
LONDON SW6 6EA ☎ 020 7736 3233
If you are looking for a historical and peaceful spot relatively nearby, the Museum of Fulham Palace and its surrounding parkland (Bishops Park), on the bank of the River Thames, may be just the thing. The site was acquired by Bishop Waldhere in 704, and the architecture is a mixture of Tudor, **Georgian** and Victorian. The gardens were used in the 17th century for breeding rare species of plants and are still beautiful today, although none of the original plants survive.

To get to Fulham Palace from Lillie Road, you will need to walk about 15–20 minutes south along Munster Road (away from Lillie Road) and then turn right on to **Fulham Road**. The nearest tube station is Putney Bridge (District line).

Fulham Road

Chelsea, South Kensington & Fulham

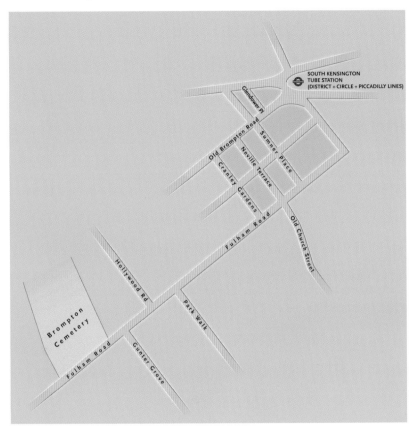

SOUTH KENSINGTON
TUBE STATION
(DISTRICT + CIRCLE + PICCADILLY LINES)

Glendower Pl

Old Brompton Road

Sumner Place

Neville Terrace

Cranley Gardens

Fulham Road

Old Church Street

Hollywood Rd

Park Walk

Brompton
Cemetery

Fulham Road

Gunter Grove

WHAT'S THERE?

'And seeing you have at Chelsea a right fair house, your library, your books, your gallery, your garden, your orchards and all other necessaries so handsomely about you, where you might, in the company of me your wife, your children, and household be merry, I muse what a God's name you mean here still thus fondly to tarry.' Thus wrote Alice, wife of Sir Thomas More (1478–1535), as he languished imprisoned for high treason in the Tower of London after refusing to accept the Act of Supremacy which established King Henry VIII as supreme head of the Church in England.

Almost 500 years later, Chelsea continues to boast 'right fair houses' and 'handsome necessaries', many of which can be found on and around Fulham Road, which has had a long relationship with the arts and artists. In the 19th century, the area had many resident artists such as James Whistler, William de Morgan, Dante Gabriel Rossetti

and Frederick Leighton, to name a few. In 1891, Whistler formed the Chelsea Arts Club, which can be found on Old Church Street, for like-minded artists, musicians and architects.

Together with **Mayfair**, the northern stretch of Fulham Road offers the very best of English antiques from the late 17th to early 19th century, including Queen Anne, Chippendale, Sheraton and Regency styles. You will also find some Irish, French and Italian antiques, all of the highest quality, and a branch of the eminent interior designers called Colefax & Fowler, all catering to the affluence and interest in the arts that characterize the neighbourhood.

WHEN IS IT OPEN?

Shops on Fulham Road typically open from 9.30 a.m. to 5.30 p.m. Monday to Friday. Some shops will open on Saturday, but it is always wise to call ahead. As shops here tend to be run by one person, you will find that many close for an hour at lunch.

HOW TO GET THERE

If you are intending to browse, take the tube to South Kensington station (District, Circle and Piccadilly lines). At the station, go through the ticket barrier and up the stairs, turning left at the top of the stairs. Outside the station, cross over the traffic island which is straight ahead of you (and pass one of the best value flower-sellers in London). On the other side of the traffic island, you will find Robert Miller Fine Art in Glendower Place (see page 20). Walk down Old Brompton Road past **Christie's** Auction House and turn left on to Cranley Gardens. At the other end of Cranley Gardens, you will hit Fulham Road at the heart of the action.

To arrive by bus, use the 14 or 414 which both pass through Hyde Park Corner and Knightsbridge, or the 345 which starts at South Kensington tube station. Alternatively, get a cab to the corner of Sydney Street and Fulham Road.

HIGHLIGHTS

Fine English antiques are presented in elegant and sophisticated settings.

LOWLIGHTS

The prices! If the western end of Fulham Road is beyond your budget, don't let it put you off. The majority of dealers will welcome you. Treat the minority that don't as sport. Be warned, however: after feasting your eyes on the exquisite, you may come back down to earth with a bump.

WHERE TO GO

Fulham Road is long and staggering in its diversity. Therefore, listings have been divided roughly into three sections by area: sw3, the western tip of the street (tube: South Kensington, District, Circle and Piccadilly lines), sw10, the very heart of Fulham Road, and eastwards along to sw6 (tube: Parsons Green, District line).

Robert Miller Fine Art 15 GLENDOWER PLACE,
LONDON SW7 3DR ✆ 020 7584 4733

The astute will notice that this is neither on Fulham Road nor in SW3; however, it is on the way for those arriving by tube and a worthy diversion for those more fortunate. From country to modernist, to pure 18th century, there will be something which appeals to you. Robert Miller's prices are very reasonable for pieces of this quality.

Hemisphere 173 FULHAM ROAD,
LONDON SW3 6JW ✆ 020 7581 9800

One of the new types of antique shops, Hemisphere displays the cool, clean lines of mostly 1920s and 1930s furniture and objects for an ultra-sophisticated and stylish European look.

Gordon Watson 50 FULHAM ROAD, LONDON SW3 6HH ✆ 020 7589 3108

In his smart and stylish gallery, Gordon Watson creates a cool and thoroughly modernist look with modern designs from the 1920s to the 1950s.

David Gill 60 FULHAM ROAD, LONDON SW3 6HH ✆ 020 7589 5946

This style-setter on Fulham Road taps into the increasing interest in 20th-century design and works of art. From Cocteau to Giacometti, David Gill is SW3's stop for modernism and **contemporary** design.

Anthony James & Son 88 FULHAM ROAD, LONDON SW3 6HR
✆ 020 7584 1120 *www.anthony-james.com*

This Fulham Road staple has fine English, French and Italian 18th- and 19th-century furniture displayed with care and charm to give a beautiful and elegant look to anyone's collection.

Michael Hughes UPSTAIRS AT 88 FULHAM ROAD,
LONDON SW3 6HR ✆ 020 7589 0660

Michael specializes in the finest English 18th- and early 19th-century furniture for the connoisseur and collector. Pieces here are of the very highest quality in terms of craftsmanship, authenticity and colour.

Godson & Coles 92 FULHAM ROAD, LONDON SW3 6HR
✆ 020 7584 2200 *www.godsonandcoles.co.uk*

The eponymous two Richards have perfectly combined their knowledge and expertise to create a stylish and bold shop specializing in fine English 18th- and 19th-century furniture. Revitalizing touches are added with modern art and textiles. This stylish shop brings a modern attitude to the world of antiques.

O. F. Wilson 3–6 QUEEN'S ELM PARADE, OLD CHURCH STREET,
LONDON SW3 6EJ ✆ 020 7352 9554

With French, English, Italian and Chinese export, O. F. Wilson epitomizes the English country-house look. *Toile de jouy* and soft decorative colours complement **painted** pieces and distressed gilt. This shop is an absolute joy to explore and an Aladdin's cave of charm and fun.

Old Church Galleries 98 FULHAM ROAD, LONDON SW3 6HS
℃ 020 7591 8790 *www.old-church-galleries.com*
At this delightful print gallery, everything is of a high quality, beautifully presented and organized by subject.

Peter Harrington 100 FULHAM ROAD, LONDON SW3 6HS
℃ 020 7591 0220 *www.peter-harrington-books.com*
Sister company to Old Church Galleries, at Peter Harrington you will find a wide range of rare antiquarian books, first editions and fine bindings together with J. K. Rowling and Dr Seuss original artwork and first editions.

Colefax & Fowler 110 FULHAM ROAD, LONDON SW3 6HU
℃ 020 7244 7427 *www.colefaxantiques.com*
Better known as a decorating firm (with its own line of wallpaper and fabrics and *Interior Inspirations* style book), Colefax & Fowler sells antiques which fit the relaxed English country style at this outpost of its main **Mayfair** showrooms.

Michael Foster 118 FULHAM ROAD, LONDON SW3 6HU ℃ 020 7373 3636
The very best of English 'country pile' chic. **Georgian** four-poster beds and Chippendale serpentine chests are combined with brilliant and luxurious silks and damasks. Visit for rich, opulent style and glamour.

Charles Saunders Antiques 255 FULHAM ROAD, LONDON SW3 6HY
℃ 020 7351 5242 *www.charlessaundersantiques.com*
Charles's engaging and decorative pieces stand out from the sea of brown furniture at this end of Fulham Road. **Painted** and slightly distressed furniture of a softer mode will go easily in the more modern home.

Robert Dickson & Lesley Rendall 263 FULHAM ROAD, LONDON SW3 6HY
℃ 020 7351 0330 *www.dicksonrendall-antiques.co.uk*
This husband and wife team sells smart English 18th- and early 19th-century furniture. This shop will appeal to those who like bold, formal antiques.

Apter Fredericks 265–267 FULHAM ROAD, LONDON SW3 6HY
℃ 020 7352 2188 *www.apter-fredericks.com*
Specializing in the highest-quality pieces of English 18th-century furniture, the Apter Fredericks family has run an antiques business on Fulham Road for five generations.

Peter Lipitch 120 FULHAM ROAD, LONDON SW3 6HU
℃ 020 7373 3328 *www.peterlipitch.com*
Another dynasty, the Lipitches are third-generation antique dealers of the highest calibre. Melvyn Lipitch of Peter Lipitch Ltd stocks beautifully drawn pieces of English 18th- and early 19th-century furniture which epitomize elegance and comfort.

SW10

H. W. Poulter & Son 279 FULHAM ROAD, LONDON SW10 9PZ
℃ 020 7352 7268 *www.hwpoulterandson.co.uk*
Poulter predominantly sells marble fireplaces and all that goes with them.

Babylon 301 FULHAM ROAD, LONDON SW10 9QH
📞 020 7376 7233 *www.babylonlondon.com*
Call at Babylon for cool, clean 20th-century Scandinavian modernism.

Orientation 2 PARK WALK, LONDON SW10 0AD 📞 020 7351 0234
Just off Fulham Road, this charming shop stocks mostly French 18th- and 19th-century furniture and works of art which sit well with Chinese export ware.

McWhirter 22 PARK WALK, LONDON SW10 0AQ
📞 020 7351 5399 *www.jamesmcwhirter.com*
McWhirter combines various genres in clever ways and offers a flexible approach to antiques. If it is stylish, of a good quality and will add interest to an interior, James McWhirter sells it. From 18th century to 20th century and architectural fragments to ashtrays, eclectic and unexpected is the key at 22 Park Walk.

Stephen Long Antiques ALBION HOUSE, 348 FULHAM ROAD,
LONDON SW10 9UH 📞 020 7352 8226
Packed with pleasing pieces and assembled with passion, this little, reasonably priced shop is everything an old-fashioned antique shop should be. You'll find hundreds if not thousands of pieces of English porcelain and ceramics.

SW6

Mark Maynard Antiques 651 FULHAM ROAD/2A CASSIDY ROAD,
LONDON SW6 5PU 📞 020 7731 3533 *www.markmaynard.co.uk*
A typical neighbourhood antique shop, Mark Maynard offers mostly white **painted French** furniture and decorative accessories.

Judy Greenwood Antiques 657–659 FULHAM ROAD,
LONDON SW6 5PY 📞 020 7736 6037
For a large selection of very pretty French decorative pieces, chandeliers, beds and textiles at reasonable prices, Judy Greenwood is a gem. This is a great find for decorating all the rooms of your home.

WHERE TO EAT

Anglesea Arms 15 SELWOOD TERRACE, LONDON SW7 3QG 📞 020 7373 7960
This is a classic yet genteel English pub with an authentic Victorian interior. In sunny weather, the Anglesea Arms is hugely popular with locals, and you'll often find antique dealers basking in the sunshine at the picnic benches. A basic menu is offered with staples such as club sandwiches and fish and chips. Take Neville Terrace (which is the continuation of Old Church Street) off Fulham Road.

Maison Blanc 303 FULHAM ROAD, LONDON SW10 9QH 📞 020 7795 2663
Starting at the antique shops at the SW3 end of Fulham Road, you'll find this inexpensive French café-cum-bakery about half way to the Chelsea and Westminster Hospital on the left-hand side of Fulham Road. This is the perfect place for a pit stop, with tasty sandwiches, quiche and pastries, and good coffee.

Riccardo's   126 FULHAM ROAD, LONDON SW3 6HU   ℂ 020 7370 6656

The service is friendly and efficient at this wonderful Italian restaurant located on the corner of Elm Place. If you can't find what you want on the large and varied menu, Riccardo's will always endeavour to whip something up to order. During summer and spring, sit out in the covered terrace and watch the world go by.

WHILE YOU'RE IN THE AREA

Brompton Cemetery   THE ROYAL PARKS, CHAPEL OFFICE,
BROMPTON CEMETERY, FULHAM ROAD, LONDON SW10 9UG
ℂ 020 7352 1201 *www.royalparks.gov.uk*

If you're going down to the sw6/sw10 end of Fulham Road, consider ordering a take-away sandwich or similar (perhaps from Maison Blanc) to eat in Brompton Cemetery. You will be emulating a popular Victorian pastime of picnicking in the cemetery, which epitomizes London's preoccupation with death at that time. The formal layout and monuments record the resting place of many notable figures of the 19th century – including American Sioux Indian Chief Long Wolf, who died while touring Europe with Buffalo Bill's Wild West Show.

Victoria & Albert Museum   CROMWELL ROAD, SOUTH KENSINGTON,
LONDON SW7 2RL ℂ 020 7942 2000 *www.vam.ac.uk*

London's design shrine is just the other side of South Kensington (District, Circle and Piccadilly lines) tube station. In 1851, 'The Great Exhibition of the Works of Industry of all Nations' was held in Hyde Park. The Exhibition showcased decorative arts with the specific purpose of promoting good design. The land on which the Victoria & Albert Museum, the Science Museum and the Natural History Museum all stand was purchased with the money raised from that very profitable exhibition. Decorative arts from the Great Exhibition eventually formed the core of what is today the Victoria & Albert Museum. To get there, take the tube to South Kensington and follow the signs, which will lead you through an underpass directly to the steps of the V&A.

Brompton Cross

At the top of Fulham Road towards Brompton Road, where Fulham Road meets Sloane Avenue, you will find one of the trendiest and smartest shopping areas in London. Located in the gorgeous **Art Deco** mosaic Michelin building, the Conran Shop exudes its ever-prevalent modern and accessible design. Also in the design category, you will find Kelly Hoppen's Life Style Emporium at 175–177 Fulham Road, specializing in all the accoutrements for the **contemporary** home. If boutique fashion is more your cup of tea, you can stop at Jimmy Choo or Betsey Johnson (at 169 and 106 Draycott Avenue respectively). At 270 and 309 Brompton Road you will find Issey Miyake and Paul & Joe.

KING'S ROAD CHELSEA

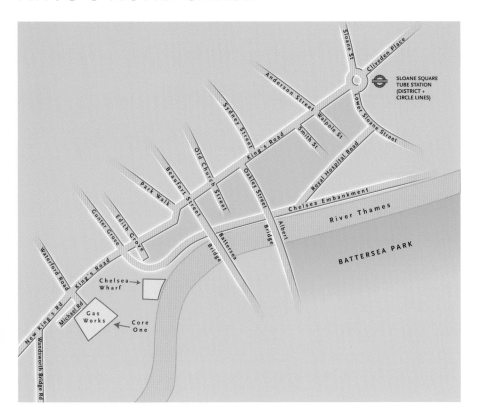

WHAT'S THERE?

Once King Charles II's private road from Whitehall to Hampton Court Palace, King's Road has historically housed a good mix of the avant-garde and the establishment. In the 18th century, cutting-edge tastes of the day were catered to by the Chelsea Porcelain Factory, located just south of King's Road along the banks of the Thames.

King's Road re-established this reputation during its 1960s heyday, when it became the spiritual home of London's 'swinging sixties'. Today, it epitomizes a mix of fresh and traditional items and houses a swathe of antique dealers who join in the sale of style to the rich and famous. Don't be scared by the headline prices: there are still finds to be found and style ideas to collect from the cool kids on King's Road.

WHEN IS IT OPEN?

King's Road shops open Monday to Friday from about 10 a.m. until 5.30–6 p.m. Many shops will open on Saturday but, as always with antique shops, it is wise to call ahead.

HOW TO GET THERE

As you exit Sloane Square (District and Circle lines) tube station, King's Road is straight ahead of you on the other side of the square. Cross the square and continue to the Peter Jones department store, which is on your right. The antique shops are spread out over the next mile and a half. To arrive by bus, take the 11 from the City of London or Victoria, or the 22, which starts at Piccadilly Circus.

HIGHLIGHTS

King's Road is possibly England's most stylish street for antiques, interiors, fashion, gifts and accessories.

LOWLIGHTS

Traffic can be unbearably slow and the streets congested.

WHERE TO GO

Antiquarius 131–141 KING'S ROAD, LONDON SW3 4PW ℂ 020 7351 5353
At this upmarket antiques arcade the dealers sell a range of stock, including luggage, ceramics, silver, jewelry and Chinese objects. A particularly stylish dealer, The Art Deco Pavilion, sells what else, but **Art Deco**.

Bourbon-Hanby Antique Centre 151 SYDNEY STREET,
LONDON SW3 6NT ℂ 020 7352 2106
Just off King's Road is this smart and appealing antiques centre with offerings of many dealers, including ceramics, glass, traditional English furniture, Chinese porcelain and 19th- and 20th-century lighting. This is the perfect one stop shop for an elegant range of small antiques.

Joanna Booth 247 KING'S ROAD, LONDON SW3 5EL
ℂ 020 7352 8998 *www.joannabooth.co.uk*
Slightly detached from the main antiques area, Joanna Booth is a good call for fine country antiques, ecclesiastical pieces and antique textiles including tapestry. Think medieval castle.

M. Charpentier Antiques 498 KING'S ROAD,
LONDON SW10 0LE ℂ 020 7351 1442
There is not a revival or repaint in sight at this American purveyor of charming, special pieces of English and French furniture. Charpentier's focus on pure antiques proves that the decorative look can be achieved with authentic pieces from the 18th and early 19th centuries.

Carlton Davidson 507 KING'S ROAD,
LONDON SW10 0TX ℂ 020 7795 0905
Carlton Davidson stocks French furniture, chandeliers, metalwork and marble in true King's Road style.

Jean Brown Antiques 515 KING'S ROAD,
LONDON SW10 OTX ℂ 020 7352 1575
The stronger, masculine look here includes stone, metal, wrought-iron lighting and architectural pieces.

L'Encoignure 517 KING'S ROAD, LONDON SW10 OTX
ℂ 020 7351 6465 *www.thomaskerrantiques.com*
Rustic French furniture and paintings fill this appealing, decorative shop.

The Furniture Cave 533 KING'S ROAD, LONDON SW10 OTZ
ℂ 020 7352 4229 *www.furniturecave.co.uk*
A Chelsea outpost for traditional and continental furniture spanning several centuries is one of London's largest and most upmarket antiques centres. 'The Cave' can take half a day of your time in itself, making it perfect if you only want to make one stop in Chelsea's antiques district or on a rainy day. Inside you will find decorative objects from the Grand Tour, antique brass, French, **Georgian** and country furniture, chandeliers and lamps, sculpture, **Art Deco**, **Asian** and modernist pieces. (There's a smart bathroom on the first floor for weary Furniture Cave shoppers.)

Langfords Marine Antiques THE PLAZA, 535 KING'S ROAD, LONDON SW10 OSZ
ℂ 020 7351 4881 *www.langfords.co.uk*
This is a great stop for the antiquarian and sailing enthusiast alike.

David Martin-Taylor Antiques 558 KING'S ROAD, LONDON SW6 2DZ
ℂ 020 7731 4135 *www.davidmartintaylor.com*
This showroom is jam-packed with everything extraordinary, including traditional, colonial, oriental and **rustic** furniture and objects.

Old World Trading Co. 565 KING'S ROAD,
LONDON SW6 2EB ℂ 020 7731 4708
For all of your antique fireplace and mantel needs, Old World has a good selection along with fireplace accoutrements and metal lighting.

Tatiana Tafur 572 KING'S ROAD, LONDON SW6 2DY ℂ 020 7731 3777
Visit Tatiana Tafur for **Art Deco** and modernist pieces with absolute glamour.

Guinevere 574–580 KING'S ROAD, LONDON SW6 2DY
ℂ 020 7736 2917 *www.guinevere.co.uk*
This King's Road staple helps make the street the beefy style Mecca that it is. Guinevere has absolutely everything and anything you could want in antiques: traditional, colonial, French, modern, **Asian** and **rustic** pieces, all displayed in a lavish, ornate setting. Red, blue and green are each shown together with elaborate displays, including walls of cut Regency glass and a fully laden dining table. A marvellous, ever-changing collection awaits at Guinevere.

Charles Edwards 582 KING'S ROAD, LONDON SW6 2DY
ℂ 020 7736 8490 *www.charlesedwards.com*
BADA dealer Charles Edwards stocks period and reproduction lighting alongside traditional 18th- and 19th-century furniture.

Mora & Upham 584 KING'S ROAD,
LONDON SW6 2DX ✆ 020 7731 4444
Exuding French glamour, Mora & Upham packs this formal and sumptuous shop with Neo-Classical furniture, ormolu and chandeliers.

Julia Boston 588 KING'S ROAD, LONDON SW6 2DX
✆ 020 7610 6783 *www.juliaboston.com*
Julia Boston commands attention with an extravagance of large and impressive 18th- and 19th-century furniture and art with real decorative appeal.

Nicole Fabre French Antiques 592 KING'S ROAD, LONDON SW6 2DX
✆ 020 7384 3112 *www.nicolefabre.co.uk*
Catering to the Fulham taste for all that is soft and pretty, Nicole Fabre sells **French painted** antiques mixed with French provincial and Venetian mirrors, all of which sit well with the vintage look textiles used in the shop.

Ossowski 595 KING'S ROAD, LONDON SW6 2EL ✆ 020 7731 0334
Glimmering from across the street, Ossowski is a specialist in antique giltwood furniture, mirrors and wall appliqués. Visit for golden glamour of the highest quality. Also on **Pimlico Road** (▶ 38).

Pimpernel & Partners 596 KING'S ROAD,
LONDON SW6 2DX ✆ 020 7731 2448
Interior design business Pimpernel & Partners also sells attractive, **painted** English and **French** pieces along with garden furniture and traditional tickings.

House of Mirrors 597 KING'S ROAD,
LONDON SW6 2EL ✆ 020 7736 5885
Here you will find 19th- and 20th-century gilt mirrors for decorating your home as well as selected furniture.

U Gütlin Clocks & Antiques 606 KING'S ROAD, LONDON SW6 2DX
✆ 020 7384 2439 *www.gutlin.com*
U Gütlin specializes in French mantel and longcase clocks and also sells ormolu objects and French furniture.

Rankin & Conn 608 KING'S ROAD, LONDON SW6 2DX
✆ 020 7384 1847 *www.rankin-conn-chinatrade.com*
A specialist dealer in Chinese and Japanese export porcelain from the 17th to the 19th century, call here for blue and white and famille rose.

Rupert Cavendish Antiques 610 KING'S ROAD, LONDON SW6 2DX
✆ 020 7731 7041 *www.rupertcavendish.co.uk*
Cavendish sells the smart streamlined look of the Empire, Biedermeier and **Art Deco** furniture and works of art. It's all about formality and style at 610.

Gallery Chelminski 616 KING'S ROAD, LONDON SW6 2DU
✆ 020 7384 2227 *www.chelminski.com*
More an art gallery than an antique dealer, grand, formal sculpture and stone garden ornaments fill this shop.

Christopher Jones Antiques 618–620 KING'S ROAD, LONDON SW6 2DU
© 020 7731 4655 *www.christopherjonesantiques.co.uk*
The eclectic mix of 18th- and 19th-century English and continental furniture, chandeliers and stone make this an elegant, charming and tempting shop.

I & JL Brown 632 & 636 KING'S ROAD, LONDON SW6 2DU
© 020 7736 4141 *www.brownantiques.com*
A true King's Road shop, I & JL Brown offers an impressive selection of English country and French provincial antiques with matching reproduction accessories.

Core One THE GASWORKS, GATE D, 2 MICHAEL ROAD,
LONDON SW6 2AN © 020 7371 5700
Just off King's Road and five minutes' walk from Michael Road, you will see an industrial estate which you wouldn't think to enter, but do. Follow the trail of signs for Core One, which will lead you through the estate to a 1970s gasworks laboratory. Here you will find six dealers who are revolutionizing the world of antiques with a perfect mix of period, quality, theatrical and **contemporary** style.

Plinth CORE ONE, THE GASWORKS, GATE D, 2 MICHAEL ROAD,
LONDON SW6 2AN © 020 7371 7422 *www.plinth.net*
Plinth stocks a phenomenal array of imposing and enticing pieces with a well-worn English or Irish country-house feel. Threadbare but fabulous upholstery clings to these well-loved pieces in a store where bold style is the theme.

Dean Antiques CORE ONE, THE GASWORKS, GATE D, 2 MICHAEL ROAD,
LONDON SW6 2AN © 020 7610 6997
Selling a theatrical mix of **painted**, modern and bold, brown period pieces, Dean Antiques is a veritable haven for the design eye looking for imposing, eclectic style.

DNA Design CORE ONE, THE GASWORKS, GATE D, 2 MICHAEL ROAD,
LONDON SW6 2AN © 020 7751 0022
DNA displays a totally modern approach to design and antiques with its energized mix of styles, materials and periods. In the world of antiques, this is cutting edge.

De Parma CORE ONE, THE GASWORKS, GATE D, 2 MICHAEL ROAD,
LONDON SW6 2AN © 07976 280 275 *www.deparma.com*
At De Parma you will find today's style and tomorrow's antiques with the highest-quality offerings from the 1920s to the 1970s.

Roderic Haugh Antiques CORE ONE, THE GASWORKS,
GATE D, 2 MICHAEL ROAD, LONDON SW6 2AN © 020 7371 5700
Bold English and French formal pieces are mixed with anything that has suitable flair or humour (including **Arts & Crafts** and modern) for a cool, confident look.

Jamb, Roger Muirhead CORE ONE, THE GASWORKS, GATE D, 2 MICHAEL ROAD,
LONDON SW6 2AN © 020 7736 3006 *www.jamblimited.com*
For your perfect reproduction English fireplaces and period, English furniture, think of Jamb. Beautiful, bold, elegant and country pieces are mixed confidently with antiquarian, modern and Grand Tour objects in a collection that displays old-fashioned cool Britannia.

Decorative Living 55 NEW KING'S ROAD, LONDON SW6 4SE
℗ 020 7736 5623 *www.decorativeliving.co.uk*
A bonanza for the astute shopper, this charming and decorative shop provides an excellent mix of periods and styles including English, French, colonial and modern pieces, all at reasonable prices.

John Clay 263 NEW KING'S ROAD, LONDON SW6 4RB ℗ 020 7731 5677
John Clay displays all things British from the 18th and 19th centuries with good humour and panache. Victorian and traditional pieces are displayed alongside stylish colonial items.

Indigo 275 NEW KING'S ROAD, LONDON SW6 4RD
℗ 020 7384 3101 *www.indigo-uk.com*
Offering stylish Eastern and oriental antiques, Indigo's furniture blends with Western antiques and the **contemporary** interior.

WHERE TO EAT

Ask Pizza & Pasta 300 KING'S ROAD, LONDON SW3 5UJ ℗ 020 7349 9123
The fresh and casual atmosphere makes Ask a perfect stop for weary shoppers. Not too busy or noisy, a range of Italian dishes under £10 are served up with polite service and in air-conditioned comfort.

Bluebird 350 KING'S ROAD, LONDON SW3 5UU ℗ 020 7559 1000
Part of the Conran empire, this sleek, stylish restaurant serves up modern British food to the design conscious.

Chutney Mary 535 KING'S ROAD, LONDON SW10 0SZ ℗ 020 7351 3113
If you are hankering after an Indian, Chutney Mary is one of London's best. Sophisticated, tasty food is served here in a smart, elegant setting.

WHILE YOU'RE IN THE AREA

Royal Hospital Chelsea ROYAL HOSPITAL ROAD, LONDON SW3 4SR
℗ 020 7881 5204 *www.chelsea-pensioners.co.uk*
The Royal Hospital Chelsea is an engaging building designed by Sir Christopher Wren (the architect of St Paul's Cathedral and countless other buildings commissioned by Charles II after the Great Fire of London in 1666). The hospital was built for those veterans of Oliver Cromwell's New Model Army who had been reduced to poverty. Step back into 17th-century London. Entry is free.

Chelsea Physic Garden 66 ROYAL HOSPITAL ROAD, LONDON SW3 4HS
℗ 020 7352 5646 *www.chelseaphysicgarden.co.uk*
At the western end of Royal Hospital Road you will find Chelsea Physic Garden, one of the oldest gardens in the world. Established in 1673 as an Apothecaries' Garden, it was formerly used for training apprentices and teaching them to identify plants. It is open from early April to late October, Wednesdays from 12 noon to 5 p.m. and Sundays from 2 p.m. to 6 p.m.

Fabulous
PIMLICO ROAD BELGRAVIA

Sloane Street

Cliveden Place

SLOANE SQUARE
TUBE STATION
(DISTRICT + CIRCLE LINES)

King's Road

Lower Sloane Street

Holbein Place

Bourne St.

Ebury Street

Pimlico Road

Dove Walk

Bloomfield Terrace

Royal Hospital Road

Chelsea Bridge Road

WHAT'S THERE?

The professional dealers on and around Pimlico Road display their wares in possibly the most stylish and impressive showrooms in London. It is the place to go for rare and unusual antiques from all over the world. Pimlico Road developed its fine reputation as an antiques hotspot relatively recently, however. Back in the 18th century, it led to Chelsea's Raneleigh Pleasure Gardens, and in the 19th century Pimlico Road became a link to Victoria mainline station. This link made it a target for extensive bombing during World War II, and in the two decades following the War this area languished as a mish-mash of pawnbrokers and bomb sites.

All of this began to change in the 1960s with the arrival of interior design and antique shop Bennison, named after founder Geoffrey Bennison. Bennison's distinctive style of faded country-house grandeur (typified by bold and often oversized furnishings and rare antique fabrics) was soon adopted by the rich and famous and gave the designer cult-like status. Following his lead more and more antique shops set up business on Pimlico Road, creating an interesting mix of quality, theatre and style. Together with its side streets and alleys, Pimlico Road now exudes a smart, village feel with over sixty dealers in antiques, art, design and other luxuries.

WHEN IS IT OPEN?

Pimlico Road is open Monday to Friday from about 10 a.m. until 5.30 p.m. On any given Saturday, only half of the shops will be open in the morning and early afternoon.

HOW TO GET THERE

Take the tube to Sloane Square (District and Circle lines). Turn left out of the station and walk down Lower Sloane Street until you get to Pimlico Road (on the left). By bus, take either the 11 from the City of London or the 211 from Waterloo, which both pass through Victoria.

HIGHLIGHTS

Quality is maintained through tough competition, making this an ideal street for ambitious designers (with hefty budgets to match).

LOWLIGHTS

Surrounded by Chelsea and Belgravia, this is not the most affordable part of London.

WHERE TO GO

Antiquus 90–92 PIMLICO ROAD, LONDON SW1W 8PL ℗ 020 7730 8681
Antiquus emulates the eclectic and formal collection of a Renaissance connoisseur. The furniture, objects and works of art on display are all chosen for their artistic merit and interest. Prepare to see Antiquus's *kunstkammer* (cabinet of curiosities) which brims with jewels, scientific instruments and more.

Blanchard 86–88 PIMLICO ROAD, LONDON SW1W 8PL ℗ 020 7823 6310
If it is interesting and stylish, Blanchard sells it. Expect the whole range, from 17th-century to more modern antiques, bold to whimsical, and traditional to exotic, all displayed with pizzazz and a sense of humour. The Pimlico Road shop is backed up by an extremely impressive showroom in Froxfield, near Marlborough in Wiltshire, only seventy miles from London.

Westenholz Antiques 76–80 PIMLICO, LONDON SW1W 8PL
℗ 020 7824 8090 *www.westenholz.co.uk*
In an extremely large gallery, Westenholz flaunts big, bold British 18th- and 19th-century antiques. This is the place to visit for robust offerings which will definitely make an impact and set the mood of a room.

Odyssey Fine Arts 24 HOLBEIN PLACE, LONDON SW1W 8NL ℗ 020 7730 9942
This gallery sells appealing 18th- and 19th-century French furniture and, in particular, **painted** Directoire pieces as well as prints, Chinese watercolours, mirrors and tole.

John Hobbs 107A PIMLICO ROAD, LONDON SW1W 8PH
℗ 020 7730 8369 *www.johnhobbs.co.uk*
One of the great names in fine antique furniture and objects, John Hobbs has an amazing showroom from which to select your Chippendale, Louis XIV, Italian Rococo and cut-crystal chandelier. To get that true country pile 'it's been in the family forever' look, be sure to call at John Hobbs.

Christopher Gibbs 3 DOVE WALK, PIMLICO ROAD, LONDON SW1W 8PH
℃ 020 7730 8200 *www.christopher-gibbs.co.uk*
Just off Pimlico Road, yet very much part of the Pimlico Road scene, Christopher Gibbs houses an awe-inspiring collection in a semi-industrial showroom. The remarkable and eclectic offerings comprise mostly rare and important pieces of English furniture and art, and you will leave Christopher Gibbs feeling as though you've 'discovered' something very special.

John King 74 PIMLICO ROAD, LONDON SW1W 8LS ℃ 020 7730 0427
John King's gallery commands your attention with its opulent and masculine look. The strength here is in early English and continental furniture and old master works of art mixed with some excellent 20th-century pieces.

Chelsea Antique Mirrors 72 PIMLICO ROAD,
LONDON SW1W 8LS ℃ 020 7824 8024
This gallery sells mostly antique gilt mirrors as well as lamps, wall appliqués and some small furniture.

Ciancimino 99 PIMLICO ROAD, LONDON SW1W 8PH
℃ 020 7730 9950 *www.ciancimino.com*
Ciancimino focuses on the clean lines and forms of **Art Deco** furniture often attributed to specific designers. The look is complemented by classically inspired 18th- and 19th-century and **Asian** decorative arts. The cool and elegant look reigns supreme at Ciancimino.

Hermitage Antiques 97 PIMLICO ROAD, LONDON SW1W 8PH
℃ 020 7730 1973 *www.hermitage-antiques.co.uk*
Hermitage Antiques sells formal, continental antiques of the Empire and Biedermeier period with a focus on Russian antiques. There is also a range of paintings and works of art to create a complete mood of Neo-Classical formality.

Nicholas Gifford-Mead 68 PIMLICO ROAD, LONDON SW1W 8LS
℃ 020 7730 6233 *www.nicholasgiffordmead.co.uk*
Nicholas Gifford-Mead stocks fireplace surrounds and sculpture, placing a strong emphasis on originality and antiquity.

Ross Hamilton 95 PIMLICO ROAD, LONDON SW1W 8PH ℃ 020 7730 3015
Ross Hamilton sells opulent continental and English antiques from the 17th to the 19th century. You will also find paintings, sculpture and other works of art.

Anno Domini Antiques 66 PIMLICO ROAD,
LONDON SW1W 8LS ℃ 020 7730 5496
A gallery displaying well-chosen pieces with space and elegance, Anno Domini carries a range of periods from 17th- to 18th-century English, as well as charming, smaller pieces which are quite affordable for the new collector.

Mark Ransom 62–64 AND 105 PIMLICO ROAD, LONDON SW1W 8LS
℃ 020 7259 0220 *www.markransom.co.uk*
Ransom specializes in glamorous, Neo-Classical style and houses a very large stock of 18th- and 19th-century continental and Russian furniture and sculpture.

Christopher Howe 93 PIMLICO ROAD, LONDON SW1W 8PH

℡ 020 7730 7987 *www.howelondon.com*

With an interesting mixture of honest and unpretentious English antiques, including **Arts & Crafts** and **rustic** pieces, Christopher Howe caters to the relaxed, elegant and pared-down interior. The focus is on good design rather than any particular period.

Christopher Hodsoll (including Bennison) 89–91 PIMLICO ROAD,

LONDON SW1W 8PH ℡ 020 7730 3370 *www.hodsoll.com*

This sumptuous gallery displays fine English 18th- and 19th-century antiques with the mood of an eccentric and theatrical country house. There are also continental pieces, and everything is presented with glamour and good humour. This is antiques at its coolest. Don't miss it!

Ossowski 83 PIMLICO ROAD, LONDON SW1W 8PH ℡ 020 7730 3256

Glimmering from across the street, Ossowski is a specialist in antique giltwood furniture, mirrors and wall appliqués. Visit for golden glamour of the best quality. There is also a branch on **King's Road** (▶ 30).

Keshishian 73 PIMLICO ROAD, LONDON SW1W 8NE

℡ 020 7730 8810 *www.keshishiancarpets.com*

If you are looking for a particularly special antique carpet, Keshishian is the place for you with tapestries, Aubussons, **Arts & Crafts** and **Art Deco** carpets.

Lamberty Antiques 46 PIMLICO ROAD, LONDON SW1W 8LP

℡ 020 7823 5115 *www.lamberty.co.uk*

Lamberty sells glamorous, bold antiques which are not confined to any particular period. Expect anything from a Roman bust to a piece of excellent 1970s design. This is one of the best **new school** antique shops. The eclectic stock is drawn together only by its quality, interest, design and style.

Christopher Butterworth Antiques 71 PIMLICO ROAD,

LONDON SW1W 8NE ℡ 020 7823 4554

Christopher Butterworth's premises are packed with antique lighting, mirrors, objects and sculpture.

Andi Gisel 69 PIMLICO ROAD, LONDON SW1W 8NE ℡ 020 7730 4187

If you're looking for elegance, Andi Gisel is your call with 19th- and early 20th-century French furniture and decorative objects, all presented with absolute refinement.

Alexander von Moltke 46 BOURNE STREET, LONDON SW1W 8JD

℡ 020 7730 9020 *www.alexandervonmoltke.com*

'Stylish' is the keyword here, where **Art Deco** sits with modernist 20th-century continental furniture, mirrors, lighting and glass, and everything is epitomized by clean lines and strong design. In the relatively new genre of 20th-century antiques, Alexander von Moltke is known for offering some of the finest pieces available.

Humphrey Carrasco 43 PIMLICO ROAD, LONDON SW1W 8NE ℡ 020 7730 9911

Masculine and cool, Humphrey Carrasco sells the country-house look with modern attitude. Expect to be captivated by the best of Britain (1700–1900) at this friendly and approachable shop.

Nicolas Guedroitz 24 PIMLICO ROAD,
LONDON SW1W 8UT ✆ 020 7730 3111
Expect high-quality Russian antiques and works at this specialist dealer.

André de Cacqueray 227 EBURY STREET,
LONDON SW1W 8UT ✆ 020 7730 5000
As well as offering interior design services, André de Cacqueray sells a range of continental antiques from the 18th and 19th centuries.

Appley Hoare Antiques 30 PIMLICO ROAD, LONDON SW1W 8LJ
✆ 020 7730 7070 *www.appleyhoare.com*
For pretty and feminine antiques, look no further than Appley Hoare where you will find **French** country **painted** furniture as well as garden accoutrements, chandeliers, metalwork and antique linens.

Gallery 25 26 PIMLICO ROAD, LONDON SW1W 8LJ ✆ 020 7730 7516
Gallery 25 is packed with a wide range of funky and unusual 20th-century furniture and decorative arts. Look beyond the chaos, and you will see why this is a favourite with dealers and designers from London and abroad.

Nigel Bartlett 22 PIMLICO ROAD, LONDON SW1W 8LJ ✆ 020 7730 3223
Nigel Bartlett stocks antique chimney pieces and works of art to give your home the architectural basics of a period look.

Bob Lawrence Gallery 93 LOWER SLOANE STREET,
LONDON SW1W 8DA ✆ 020 7730 5900
This gallery, just off Pimlico Road, sells 20th-century pieces which exemplify modernism. Expect fabulous **Art Deco** and all its accoutrements.

Peta Smyth 42 MORETON STREET, LONDON SW1V 2PB ✆ 020 7630 9898
One of the best dealers in antique textiles and carpets, there is always something beautiful and rare at Peta Smyth.

WHERE TO EAT

La Poule au Pot 231 EBURY STREET, LONDON SW1W 8UT ✆ 020 7730 7763
The next best thing to nipping to Paris for lunch, this upmarket and intimate French restaurant also boasts an excellent terrace for taking in the comings and goings of this busy street on warm days.

The Ebury 11 PIMLICO ROAD, LONDON SW1W 8NA
✆ 020 7730 6784 *www.theebury.co.uk*
With a brassiere/lounge on the ground floor and more formal dining room on the first, The Ebury serves gourmet food from some of Britain's best chefs in suitably elegant surroundings just on Pimlico Road.

Flamenco 54 PIMLICO ROAD, LONDON SW1W 8LP ✆ 020 7730 4484
For good Spanish fare try Flamenco. It is in the heart of the antiques district and offers fresh food and friendly service.

WHILE YOU'RE IN THE AREA

Linley 60 PIMLICO ROAD, LONDON SW1W 8LP ✆ 020 7730 7300
Buy tomorrow's antiques today at Linley. As well as being the Queen's nephew and twelfth in line to the throne, David Linley is currently one of England's most eminent furniture makers.

Carlyle's House 24 CHEYNE ROW, LONDON SW3 5HL ✆ 020 7352 7087
www.nationaltrust.org.uk/places/carlyleshouse
On Cheyne Row you will find a beautiful early 18th-century house which served as Thomas Carlyle's residence during the 19th century. Carlyle is recognized as one of the greatest writers of the Victorian age and was friends with contemporary writers including Tennyson, Dickens, Ruskin and Darwin, who were all frequent visitors to this address. The house is filled with Carlyle's personal possessions and gives a great feel for the Victorian interior. It opens April to October on Wednesdays, Thursdays and Fridays (2–5 p.m.), and Saturdays, Sundays and Bank Holidays (11 a.m.–5 p.m.).

Royal Hospital Chelsea ROYAL HOSPITAL ROAD, LONDON SW3 4SR
✆ 020 7881 5204 *www.chelsea-pensioners.co.uk* ▶ 32

Chelsea Physic Garden 66 ROYAL HOSPITAL ROAD, LONDON SW3 4HS
✆ 020 7352 5646 *www.chelseaphysicgarden.co.uk* ▶ 32

St James's

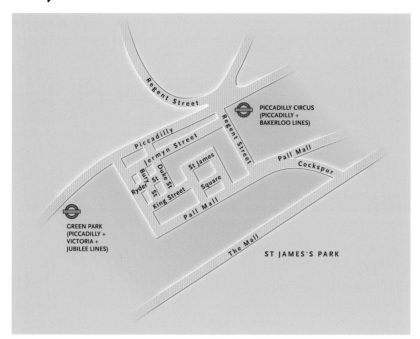

PICCADILLY CIRCUS
(PICCADILLY +
BAKERLOO LINES)

Regent Street

Piccadilly

Jermyn Street

Bury St

Duke St

Ryder St

St James

St James
Square

King Street

Pall Mall

Regent Street

Pall Mall

Cockspur

GREEN PARK
(PICCADILLY +
VICTORIA +
JUBILEE LINES)

The Mall

ST JAMES'S PARK

WHAT'S THERE?

Looking at the St James's area, it is hard to believe that the beautiful park for which it is now renowned was once a swampy meadow. These days, St James's Park and Palace form the heart and focal point of this particularly 'London' neighbourhood.

The palace was built by Henry VIII in the 16th century on the site of a 12th-century Lepers' hospital, and the swampland was turned into a nursery for deer. The area was still quite wild until the late 1600s, however. It was during this period that Charles II asked Le Notre to landscape the grounds, and rumour has it that the park became a regular meeting place for him and his mistress Nell Gwynne.

Later, St James's catered for wealthy gentlemen, particularly those who were associated with the palace, and it remains home to many traditional shops selling gentlemanly things such as cigars, guns, shirts, handmade shoes and art. **Christie's** main auction house has been just around the corner since the 18th century, which has meant that the art and antiques lover has never had to travel far within St James's for all the accoutrements of courtly life.

Bound by Piccadilly, Pall Mall, Green Park and Lower Regent Street, St James's is a step back into the world of the 18th-century gentleman collector. The galleries, as antique stores are more appropriately known in this neighbourhood, sell only the highest-quality paintings, sculpture, furniture and **Asian** works of art. This is not the place to go if you're on a budget or scruffily dressed.

WHEN IS IT OPEN?

The galleries of St James's are open from 10 a.m. until 5 p.m. Monday to Friday.

HOW TO GET THERE

By tube, you can go to either Green Park (Piccadilly, Jubilee and Victoria lines) or Piccadilly Circus (Bakerloo and Piccadilly lines). Piccadilly (street), which runs between the two stations, marks out the northern boundary of St James's. You can also take a bus to Piccadilly Circus and/or Green Park from almost anywhere in London as they are the main hubs of London transport. The 14 from South Kensington and the 11 from **King's Road** both go to Green Park and are particularly useful for connecting the antiques areas. If you are travelling by taxi, ask for the corner of Jermyn Street and Bury Street.

HIGHLIGHTS

St James's exudes old-world mood, charm and quality.

LOWLIGHTS

St James's formal atmosphere and high-end prices can be intimidating. Worry not, however, as part of St James's charm is impeccable manners.

WHERE TO GO

Harris Lindsay 67 JERMYN STREET, LONDON SW1Y 6NY ℭ 020 7839 5767
At Harris Lindsay you will find the epitome of a tasteful St James's gallery. You must know where you are going as there is no shop front, but once inside, you will find a large selection of the finest-quality English antique furniture and objects, all beautifully presented. This is a true connoisseur's call, with museum quality and a private atmosphere.

Trevor Philip & Sons 75A JERMYN STREET, LONDON SW1Y 6NP
ℭ 020 7930 2954 *www.trevorphilip.com*
Befitting a gentlemen's shopping street, this gentlemen's antique shop stocks antique globes and early scientific instruments.

Brian Harkins 3 BURY STREET, LONDON SW1Y 6AB ℭ 020 7839 3338
Brian Harkins sells the best of **Asian** refinement with his selection of Chinese and Japanese works of art.

John Bly 27 BURY STREET, LONDON SW1Y 6AL ℭ 07831 888 825 *www.johnbly.com*
John Bly is a fifth-generation fine antique dealer with premises in Tring, Hertfordshire, where the first shop was established, and in St James's. Bly is a regular contributor to the *Antiques Roadshow* as well as author of several books on English antiques, so quality is assured. Bly and staff are friendly and kind despite the shop being open by appointment only.

Albert Amor 37 BURY STREET, LONDON SW1Y 6AU *www.albertamor.co.uk*
Visit this gorgeous gallery which purveys the finest 18th-century English porcelain to salubrious clients including H. M. the Queen and the like.

Jonathan Tucker Antonia Tozer Asian Art 37 BURY STREET, LONDON SW1Y 6AU
℡ 020 7839 3414 *www.asianartresource.co.uk*
Again, more art than antiques, this St James's gallery sells museum-quality **Asian** works of art, including ceramics, furniture, carpets and remarkable sculpture.

Malcolm Fairley 40 BURY STREET,
LONDON SW1Y 6AU ℡ 020 7930 8770
The flavour of St James's is reflected in this gallery of Japanese antiques, which specializes in metalworks, enamels, lacquer, ceramics, inro and Meiji netsuke.

John Carlton-Smith 17 RYDER STREET, LONDON SW1Y 6PY
℡ 020 7930 6622 *www.fineantiqueclocks.com*
A BADA dealer in the finest English 17th- to 19-century clocks and barometers, John Carlton-Smith selects pieces from the most renowned makers with excellent patination and in untouched carcases, creating a truly exquisite and unique collection.

Didier Aaron 21 RYDER STREET, LONDON SW1Y 6PX
℡ 020 7839 4716 *www.didieraaroninc.com*
Part of a network of galleries in Paris, New York and London, Didier Aaron sells French paintings and drawings from the 17th to the 19th century, and European furniture from the 18th to the 19th century. Everything is of the highest quality, and the galleries cater for connoisseur collectors and museums alike.

Pullman Gallery 14 KING STREET, LONDON SW1Y 6QU
℡ 020 7930 9595 *www.pullmangallery.com* ▶ 50
The original premises of Pullman Gallery sells gentlemen's collectibles (also known as *Objets de Luxe* 1880–1950), including cocktail shakers and motoring accessories.

Kenneth Davis 15 KING STREET, LONDON SW1Y 6QU ℡ 020 7930 0313
A fine selection of Chinese ceramics and works of art awaits.

Priestley & Ferraro 17 KING STREET, LONDON SW1Y 6QU
℡ 020 7930 6228 *www.priestleyandferraro.com*
A top-end dealer in Song ceramics and early Chinese art, Priestley & Ferraro sells pieces which are works of art in their own right.

Simon Ray Indian & Islamic Works of Art 21 KING STREET, LONDON SW1Y 6QY
℡ 020 7930 5500 *www.simonray.com*
More art gallery than antique shop, Simon Ray has a stunning stock of Indian and Islamic arts, including Iznik tiles, Mohgal metal and stone, beautiful sculpture and amazing miniatures.

Asian Art Gallery – Christopher Bruckner 8 DUKE STREET,
LONDON SW1Y 6BN ℡ 020 7930 0204
In a real gallery setting, you will find pieces from China, Japan and Tibet for sale with a speciality in Imperial Tibetan.

WHERE TO EAT

Just St James 12 ST JAMES STREET, LONDON SW1A 1ER ℂ 020 7976 2222
Just Oriental 19 KING STREET, LONDON SW1Y 6QU ℂ 020 7930 9292
www.juststjames.com
Two sister establishments sit a few yards from each other on King Street: the upmarket Just St James and the oriental bar/brassiere Just Oriental. Main courses at Just St James tend to be in the £10–20 bracket, and at Just Oriental around £7–10. Just Oriental has an intimate, sophisticated atmosphere and a tasty lunch menu. Both restaurants are particularly close to **Christie's** King Street auction rooms.

Franco's Restaurant & Mokaris 61–63 JERMYN STREET,
LONDON SW1Y 6LX ℂ 020 7493 3645
The two attached Italian brasseries serve a range of traditional dishes, particularly pasta. Diners can sit both inside and outside, making this a perfect stop.

Fortnum & Mason 181 PICCADILLY, LONDON W1A 1ER
ℂ 020 7734 8040 *www.fortnumandmason.com*
With several eating venues, you can choose between formal and casual to suit all tastes and budgets.

WHILE YOU'RE IN THE AREA

Jermyn Street
This gentlemen's street has real London flavour. The buildings date from the 17th century when Henry Jermyn built on land leased from the Crown. St James's Square, just off Pall Mall, housed the very well-to-do, and tradesmen set up on Jermyn Street to service this clientele. There was a bag-maker, a marine glue manufacturer, a hat-trimmer, a stay-maker, a grocer and a maker of hairbrushes. Today, Jermyn Street is best known for its shirt-makers, but it is also home to perfumers, cheese-mongers and cobblers.

Hatchard's Booksellers 187 PICCADILLY, LONDON W1J 9LE
ℂ 020 7439 9921 *www.hatchards.co.uk*
The oldest bookstore in London, Hatchard's has been open on Piccadilly since the late 18th century. Creaking floors add to the old-world atmosphere.

Fortnum & Mason 181 PICCADILLY, LONDON W1A 1ER
ℂ 020 7734 8040 *www.fortnumandmason.com*
This is old-fashioned retail therapy! The store is named after the founders – two men called Fortnum and Mason. In 1705, Fortnum met and took lodgings with Mason, who had a shop in **St James's Market**. The former became a footman to the royal household of Queen Anne and a seller of used candles. Within two years, the two had set up as grocers. The store had close associations with the East India Company and also provided boxes and baskets of food to the soldiers of the Peninsular War (1808–14). To this day, Fortnum & Mason sells luxury foods as well as other department store offerings. The beautiful building, with its traditions, formal doorman and lavish interiors, is a quintessential London experience. Be sure to view the antiques and art on the fourth floor.

Millionaire
MAYFAIR

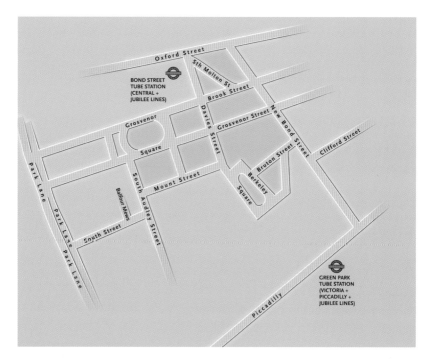

WHAT'S THERE?

Mayfair derives its name from the annual country fair which took place just north of Piccadilly until it was squeezed out by an 18th-century building boom. This development made Mayfair London's most exclusive and wealthy neighbourhood. Today, Mayfair remains quintessentially **Georgian** with elegant houses and mews. It is bordered by Piccadilly to the south, with its Royal Academy of Arts; Bond Street to the east, with its exclusive jewelry shops and auction houses; Park Lane to the west, where the most expensive and exclusive London palaces once stood; and by the thronging shops of Oxford Street to the north.

Catering for its wealthy residents and visitors, Mayfair is a goldmine of luxury. It is hard to take two steps in Mayfair without coming across an antique shop or art gallery. The main specialities are English and French furniture and **Asian** art of the highest calibre. If you really want to fit in, have the driver bring round the Bentley for your visit!

WHEN IS IT OPEN?

Mayfair's antique shops open Monday to Friday from about 10 a.m. until 5.30 p.m. Many, if not most, will be closed on Saturday.

HOW TO GET THERE

By public transport, get off at either Bond Street (Central and Jubilee lines) or Green Park (Piccadilly, Victoria and Jubilee lines) tube stations for a walk through smart Mayfair. You can take a bus to Bond Street and/or Green Park from almost anywhere in London. The 14 from South Kensington and the 11 from **King's Road** both go to Green Park and are particularly useful for connecting the antiques areas. Arriving by taxi, start at the auction rooms on Bond Street and continue to Mount Street by foot.

HIGHLIGHTS

This is authentic old London and boasts architecture that is, for the most part, pure 18th-century elegance with fan lights, wrought-iron balustrades and **Georgian** columned entrances. There are also many galleries of modern, old and **Asian** art to peruse, even if only from the pavement.

LOWLIGHTS

You can easily shave a few million off your bank balance before lunch.

WHERE TO GO

Burlington Arcade PICCADILLY, LONDON W1J 0QJ
At Burlington Arcade you will step back into Regency England in the heart of Mayfair. Built in 1818 by the Earl of Burlington, the covered shopping arcade was created 'for the sale of jewellery and fancy articles of fashionable demand'. To this day the arcade remains guarded by uniformed Beadles who enforce Regency laws, prohibiting singing, humming and hurrying in the arcade. Among its many stores, the arcade hosts a cache of antique shops selling silver, *objets de vertu* and antique jewelry. Daniel Bexfield (*www.bexfield.co.uk*) at number 26 is particularly worth a visit. His passionate enthusiasm for fine quality, patinated silver and jewelry is infectious.

Partridge Fine Art 144–146 NEW BOND STREET, LONDON W1S 2PF
℡ 020 7629 0834 *www.partridgefinearts.com*
Only the best French, English and continental antiques, textiles and works of art are sold at this formidable shop with its elegant pieces and security guard all visible from the large window frontage. Partridge has been a London institution since the turn of the century and counts many famous private collectors and renowned museums as clients.

Mallett 141 NEW BOND STREET, LONDON W1S 2BS
℡ 020 7499 7411 *www.mallett.co.uk*
If Partridge has a contender as the most elegant and expensive antique shop in London, it is Mallett. Whereas Partridge may have a formal French 18th-century signed cabinet from Marie Antoinette's boudoir, Mallett will stock the perfect piece of English Chippendale by which every other antique should be judged. Although Mallett stocks both continental and English antiques, it is the proprietor of English cabinetry at its most perfect. There is another selling venue for Mallett in an 18th-century

house called Bourdon House, 2 Davies Street, Mayfair, with displays that are more like a home than a showroom.

Ronald Phillips   26 BRUTON STREET, LONDON W1J 6LQ ℂ 020 7493 2341
This beautiful shop specializes in English 18th- and early 19th-century pieces of the highest quality. Everything here is elegant, period and befitting the best collections.

M. Turpin   27 BRUTON STREET, LONDON W1X 6QN
ℂ 020 7493 3275 www.mturpin.co.uk
M. Turpin has the finest English 18th-century antiques, with a speciality in giltwood.

Antoine Cheneviere Fine Arts   UPSTAIRS AT 27 BRUTON STREET,
LONDON W1J 6QH ℂ 020 7491 1007
Upstairs at 27 Bruton Street, you will find a salon of 18th- and 19th-century Russian, Austrian, German and Italian furniture and objects.

Victor Arwas Gallery   3 CLIFFORD STREET, LONDON W1S 2LF
ℂ 020 7734 3944 www.victorarwas.com
For the connoisseur, this gallery has a large stock of late 19th-century and early 20th-century fine and decorative arts with a particular strength in **Art Nouveau**. Victor Arwas is a published expert, lecturer and curator in the period, and often lends to museum exhibitions throughout the world.

Eskenazi   10 CLIFFORD STREET, LONDON W1S 2LH
ℂ 020 7493 5464 www.eskenazi.co.uk
Eskenazi is synonymous with museum-quality Chinese ceramics and works of art and holds some of the most impressive and authoritative exhibitions outside public museums. Experts in the most important, rare and expensive pieces should call here.

Robert Hall   15C CLIFFORD STREET, LONDON W1S 4JZ
ℂ 020 7734 4008 www.snuffbottle.com
Visit Robert Hall to see the top-end authority and dealer in antique Chinese snuff bottles. To the novice these may look like trinkets, whereas in reality they are important treasures.

Gordon Reece Gallery   16 CLIFFORD STREET, LONDON W1S 3RG
ℂ 020 7439 0007 www.gordonreecegalleries.com
This large, impressive gallery offers the perfect serene setting for antique furniture, decorative and tribal arts and architectural objects from China, Japan, India and South-East Asia. With nothing made for Western tourists at any point in time, pieces here are rare and aesthetically beautiful.

Windsor House Antiques   28–29 DOVER STREET, LONDON W1S 4NA
ℂ 020 7659 0340 www.windsorhouseantiques.co.uk
Dating back to 1957, Windsor House sells the kind of quality English antiques one would expect in Mayfair. A particular strength of this gallery is an emphasis on selling antiques with a range of prices, ensuring that the novice collector will never feel intimidated.

A & J Speelman Oriental Art 129 MOUNT STREET, LONDON W1K 3NX
© 020 7499 5126 *www.ajspeelman.com*
This third-generation antique dealer has created an oasis of **Asian** objects and art of the highest quality. The pieces here are the rarest and most unusual, and Speelman's clarity of vision soon becomes apparent. You will not see anything comparable any time soon.

Aaron Gallery 125 MOUNT STREET, LONDON W1K 3NS
© 020 7499 9434 *www.aarongallery.com*
This fourth-generation dealer in the finest Ancient antiques from the Islamic world, Near East, Greek and Roman Empires and Egypt has been an advisor to the Persian Royal Family.

Alistair Sampson Antiques 120 MOUNT STREET, LONDON W1K 3NN
© 020 7409 1799 *www.alistairsampson.com*
Upon entering this shop, you will step back three hundred years. Whereas other Mayfair dealers may have gilt and glamour befitting a sultan, Alistair Sampson's stock includes charming, English 17th-century turned tables and 16th- and 17th-century stump work and samplers. When you begin to comprehend the age of the pieces, you will be absolutely captivated even by simple walnut tables!

H. Blairman & Sons 119 MOUNT STREET, LONDON W1K 3NL
© 020 7493 0444 *www.blairman.co.uk*
Blairman specializes in the finest English 19th-century antiques, including Aesthetic and **Arts & Crafts**, all of which are selected for quality, individuality and integrity.

Pullman Gallery 116 MOUNT STREET, LONDON W1K 3NH
© 020 7499 8080 *www.pullmangallery.com*
This is one of the two venues for the Pullman Gallery which specializes in *Objets de Luxe* 1880–1950 such as cocktail shakers and motoring collectibles (including posters). There is also a branch at 14 King Street in **St James's** (▶ 44).

Gerard Hawthorn 104 MOUNT STREET, LONDON W1K 2TJ *©* 020 7409 2888
Amidst the opulence of Mayfair's furniture and art galleries, Gerard Hawthorn has created a space of **Asian** delicacy and calm with items of Chinese Ming art, ceramics, furniture and sculpture displayed with selected Japanese and Korean antiques, all of the highest quality and in the finest condition.

Riyahi Gallery 97 MOUNT STREET, LONDON W1K 2TD *©* 020 7629 0143
Riyahi Gallery is elegant with fine Ancient, Islamic and **Asian** antique works of art.

Mount Street Galleries 93 MOUNT STREET, LONDON W1K 1SY *©* 020 7493 1613
With stock impressively displayed in suitably grand premises, the look of Mount Street Galleries is undeniably masculine, bold and moody. Expect Regency, colonial and elaborate continental furniture which is striking and sumptuous.

Neame 27 MOUNT STREET, LONDON W1K 2RR *©* 020 7629 0445
An elegant connoisseur's shop which is more than worthy of its Mayfair address, Neame's Chippendale, Regency and Queen Anne pieces are evocative of the most elegant furnishings from an English palace.

Pelham Galleries 24 & 25 MOUNT STREET,
LONDON W1K 2RR © 020 7629 0905
A gorgeous gallery stocking 18th-century English and French furniture as well as Chinese export objects, Pelham also specializes in rare musical instruments.

A. Pash & Sons 37 SOUTH AUDLEY STREET,
LONDON W1K 2PN © 020 7499 5176
Extravagant silver centrepieces, chandeliers and dining-room pieces create the mood for all-out luxury.

Mayfair Gallery 39–40 SOUTH AUDLEY STREET,
LONDON W1K 2PS © 020 7491 3435
Ornate and glamorous continental furniture from the 18th and 19th centuries is displayed with antique German porcelain, French bronzes and marble busts for a flamboyant look.

Adrian Alan 66/67 SOUTH AUDLEY STREET, LONDON W1K 2QX
© 020 7495 2324 *www.adrianalan.net*
At this Mayfair gallery, the total opulence of 19th-century furniture of the highest standards of craftsmanship is on offer with a specialization in pieces from the Great Exhibitions of the 19th century.

Emanouel Corporation UK 64 & 64A SOUTH AUDLEY STREET,
LONDON W1K 2QT © 020 7493 4350 *www.emanouel.net*
Sumptuous and lavish French 19th-century furniture and works of art are sold at this large corner gallery.

Grace Wu Bruce 12A BALFOUR MEWS,
LONDON W1K 2BJ © 020 7499 3750
Grace Wu Bruce's collection of the highest-quality antique Chinese furniture promises absolute elegance and simplicity.

Colefax & Fowler 39 BROOK STREET, LONDON W1K 4JE
© 020 7493 2231 *www.colefaxantiques.com*
The Mayfair headquarters of these style gurus and creators of the true English country pile look is an absolute joy to enter. The building, the garden, the antiques, the art and the whole mood epitomize relaxed comfort and elegance. A whole range of antique furniture, art and objects is on offer and presented, of course, with total panache.

Sydney L. Moss 51 BROOK STREET, LONDON W1K 4HP
© 020 7629 4670 *www.slmoss.com*
One of the few experts in the esoteric field of Chinese literati arts (painting, calligraphy and objects to the 'scholar's taste'), Sydney Moss sells the most beautiful scrolls as well as Japanese netsuke and lacquer.

Yacob's Gallery 28 DAVIES STREET,
LONDON W1K 4NA © 020 7499 9966
This Islamic antiques specialist sells Ancient art, fine ceramics, sculpture and carpets in elegant West End style.

Hadji Baba 34A DAVIES STREET,
LONDON W1K 4NE © 020 7499 9363
For the perfect Islamic piece to crown your collection, Hadji Baba has the finest
ceramic and sculpture fragments.

Jan Van Beers Oriental Art 34 DAVIES STREET, LONDON W1K 4NE
© 020 7408 0434 www.janvanbeers.com
Fine Chinese pottery and porcelain from the Han to the Qing dynasties are imma-
culately presented at Jan Van Beers.

Gray's Antiques Markets 58 DAVIES STREET, LONDON W1K 5LP
© 020 7629 7034 www.egrays.com
In a beautiful 19th-century terracotta building, you will find Gray's, where dealers
who specialize in smaller objects of the highest quality can sell to the international
elite without enormous overheads. Quality and presentation are impeccable. Stock
includes all kinds of small decorative arts from ceramics to clocks as well as prints,
silver and **Asian** works of art. If Mayfair has left you feeling slightly intimidated, you
will be comfortable at Gray's while enjoying Mayfair quality and presentation.

WHERE TO EAT

Richoux 41A SOUTH AUDLEY STREET, LONDON W1K 2PS © 020 7629 5228
(also 171 PICCADILLY, LONDON W1V 9DD © 020 7629 4991)
Visit Richoux on South Audley Street for Mayfair elegance at reasonable prices. This
traditional French café serves everything from cakes, tea and coffee to hot lunches.

Serafino 8 MOUNT STREET, LONDON W1K 3NF © 020 7629 0544
This excellent restaurant boasts three venues. On the north side of Mount Street
there is a sandwich café downstairs and a more formal restaurant upstairs. Across the
street, at Delphino, you will find pizza and pasta, and the setting is fresh and smart.

WHILE YOU'RE IN THE AREA

Royal Academy of Arts BURLINGTON HOUSE, PICCADILLY, LONDON W1J 0BD
© 020 7300 8000 www.royalacademy.org.uk
Founded in 1768 as an institution for artists and the arts, the Royal Academy moved in
1868 to a beautiful 1720s Palladian house built by Lord Burlington. It has held annual
summer exhibitions of contemporary art since 1769. At the top of the staircase, which
is open and free to the public, there is also a gorgeous Michelangelo roundel sculpture, making this a wonderful stop even if you only have a spare ten minutes.

Liberty 210–220 REGENT STREET, LONDON W1B 5AH
© 020 7734 1234 www.liberty.co.uk
In 1875, Arthur Lasenby Liberty opened a shop selling ornaments, fabric and *objets
d'art* from Japan and the East. Liberty became hugely popular and included clients
such as Rossetti, Leighton and Burne-Jones. In the 1890s, Liberty adopted the style of
the **Arts & Crafts** and **Art Nouveau** movements. Recognizable by its Tudor-style building made from the wood of salvaged ships in 1924, Liberty remains a style innovator.

KENSINGTON CHURCH STREET
KENSINGTON

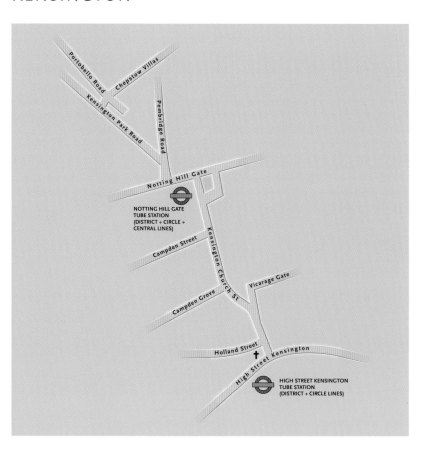

WHAT'S THERE?

Kensington Church Street's history can be found in its name: it lies on land once owned by the vicarage of Kensington. When the land was sold to property developers in 1854, the contract stipulated against occupants engaged in any trade which 'would prove hazardous, noisy or offensive....' One hundred years later, the Kensington Church Street Association turned to this contract to restrict shops on the street to retailers in the art and antiques trade or essential grocery supplies.

These days, you will find a range of furniture and objects on Kensington Church Street, including English 18th-century furniture, 19th-century grandeur and decorative arts from the mid-19th century to modernism. This is also a street for specialists of porcelain, oriental and English antiques.

WHEN IS IT OPEN?

Kensington Church Street shops open Monday to Friday from about 10 a.m. until 5.30–6 p.m. Many shops will open on Saturday, but it is wise to call ahead.

HOW TO GET THERE

Get the tube to High Street Kensington (District and Circle lines), turn right on to Kensington High Street and you will soon see a large church on the left side of the road. This marks the bottom end of Kensington Church Street. From **Notting Hill Gate** (District, Circle and Central lines) tube station, follow exit signs for Kensington Church Street and Notting Hill Gate southside. The first street on your right is Kensington Church Street. By bus, you can take the 27 from Camden or Paddington, the 52 from Victoria or Hyde Park Corner, and the 70 from South Kensington.

HIGHLIGHTS

This is a beautiful part of London, with gleaming white Victorian buildings and charming, old streets. The area is pristine and upmarket.

LOWLIGHTS

Expect traffic and crowds in this busy, touristy part of London.

WHERE TO GO

There are over fifty individual antique shops on Kensington Church Street. Listings have been divided into three categories: traditional antique shops (including furniture, objects and decorative arts), oriental specialists and ceramics.

TRADITIONAL ANTIQUE SHOPS

Roderick Antique Clocks 23 VICARAGE GATE, LONDON W8 4AA
© 020 7937 8517 *www.roderickantiqueclocks.com*
Roderick selects the finest antique clocks for their originality and wonderful colour.

Paul Reeves 32B KENSINGTON CHURCH STREET, LONDON W8 4HA
© 020 7937 1594 *www.paulreeveslondon.com*
Paul Reeves sells the highest-quality British decorative arts, including **Arts & Crafts**, Aesthetic and Gothic revival, with many signed and attributed pieces. This is a wonderful and rare opportunity for the avid collector.

Artemis Decorative Arts 36 KENSINGTON CHURCH STREET,
LONDON W8 4BX © 020 7376 0377
Clean lines and streamlined modernism are on show in this elegant gallery of 20th-century decorative arts. Artemis is where you can decorate your modernist European pad with furniture and objects in **Art Deco** and 1940s French styles.

Michael German Antiques 38B KENSINGTON CHURCH STREET,
LONDON W8 4BX © 020 7937 2771
www.antiqueweapons.com www.antiquecanes.com
Manly things for the gentleman collector can be bought at this dapper gallery, including
walking sticks, arms and armour.

Kensington Church Street Antiques Centre 58–60 KENSINGTON CHURCH
STREET, LONDON W8 4DB © 020 7376 0425
At this smart antiques centre which stocks quality pieces that befit Kensington
Church Street, several dealers offer late 19th- and early 20th-century decorative arts,
oriental works of art, painting, decorative glass, majolica, silver and jewelry.

Adrian Harrington 64A KENSINGTON CHURCH STREET, LONDON W8 4DB
© 020 7937 1465 *www.harringtonbooks.co.uk*
Adrian Harrington is a wonderful antiquarian bookseller. Step out of the modern,
busy world of Kensington into a peaceful haven of gorgeous books.

Collectable Antiques 66E KENSINGTON CHURCH STREET,
LONDON W8 4BY © 020 7229 2934
An approachable and appropriately named shop, Collectable Antiques is dedicated
to small, collectible antiques, including porcelain, prints and dolls.

Puritan Values 69 KENSINGTON CHURCH STREET, LONDON W8 4BG
© 020 7937 2410 *www.puritanvalues.co.uk*
This London branch of a Suffolk-based **Arts & Crafts** dealer sells furniture, lighting
and decorative arts. The passion for Arts & Crafts here borders on obsession, and
Puritan Values also boasts a categorial knowledge of the designers and craftsmen
who led style in Britain from 1850 to 1915.

The Lacquer Chest 71 & 75 KENSINGTON CHURCH STREET,
LONDON W8 4BG © 020 7937 1306
The two branches of this shop sell charming and interesting decorative antiques
from the 18th and 19th centuries with a **folk art** feel. You will find furniture, pictures,
ceramics and lighting, all with naive appeal.

Pruskin Gallery 50 & 73 KENSINGTON CHURCH STREET,
LONDON W8 4BG © 020 7937 1994
Only the very best, and often signed, decorative arts from 1880 to 1960 are offered
here with style and panache.

Neil Wibroe & Natasha MacIlwaine 77 KENSINGTON CHURCH STREET,
LONDON W8 4BG © 020 7937 2461
Selling fine English 18th- and early 19th-century antiques, Wibroe and MacIlwaine's
gallery has a refined and genteel mood about it.

Raffety & Walwyn 79 KENSINGTON CHURCH STREET, LONDON W8 4BG
© 020 7938 1100 *www.raffetyantiqueclocks.com*
This specialist dealer in fine clocks and barometers is run by two friendly and expert
dealers jokingly known as Tick and Tock in the trade.

Reindeer Antiques 81 KENSINGTON CHURCH STREET, LONDON W8 4BG
☎ 020 7937 3754 *www.reindeerantiques.co.uk*
This smart, elegant shop is the London branch of a Northamptonshire dealer selling the finest English 17th- to early 19th-century antiques. Reindeer captures the look of an 18th-century London town house or English country pile.

Lev 97A KENSINGTON CHURCH STREET,
LONDON W8 7LN ☎ 020 7727 9248
At this old-fashioned shop, interesting paintings, objects and jewelry can be procured, and everything has a charming, unusual look.

Eila Grahame 97C KENSINGTON CHURCH STREET,
LONDON W8 7LN ☎ 020 7727 4132
This small shop sells interesting and specially selected pieces, including English 18th- and early 19th-century furniture, paintings and other small works of art.

Brian Rolleston Antiques 104A KENSINGTON CHURCH STREET,
LONDON W8 4BU ☎ 020 7229 5892
A high-end fine English 18th-century furniture dealer, Brian Rolleston's display is spacious, allowing proper appreciation of each piece.

Haslam and Whiteway 105 KENSINGTON CHURCH STREET,
LONDON W8 7LN ☎ 020 7229 1145
This is a fabulous gallery of British decorative arts and all that was cutting edge and modern just over one hundred years ago. Expect Gothic revival, Aestheticism and excellent **Arts & Crafts**, all of good design and quality.

Eddy Bardawil 106 KENSINGTON CHURCH STREET,
LONDON W8 4BH ☎ 020 7221 3967
A gorgeous display of fine English 18th- and early 19th-century furniture and works of art is maintained by quality dealer Eddy Bardawil.

H. and W. Deutsch Antiques 111 KENSINGTON CHURCH STREET,
LONDON W8 7LN ☎ 020 7727 5984
Expect a range of smalls, including silver, ceramics, oriental and works of art.

David Brower 113 KENSINGTON CHURCH STREET, LONDON W8 7LN
☎ 020 7221 4155 *www.davidbrower-antiques.com*
A plethora of 19th-century European antiques and sculpture, as well as oriental art, is opulently displayed at David Brower.

Green's Antique Galleries 117 KENSINGTON CHURCH STREET,
LONDON W8 7LN ☎ 020 7229 9618
Romantics will love the range of antique engagement rings at this small shop which also has silver, glass and jewelry.

B. Silverman 4 CAMPDEN STREET, LONDON W8 7EP
☎ 020 7985 0555 *www.silverman-london.com*
A third-generation silver dealer with offerings from the 18th to the 20th century, B. Silverman's approach is friendly and his knowledge unquestionable.

Decor Interiors 125 KENSINGTON CHURCH STREET,
LONDON W8 7LP ✆ 020 7221 1080
With 19th-century furniture, chandeliers and porcelain, the small shop sells the
accoutrements of the feminine and traditional interior.

Through the Looking Glass 137 KENSINGTON CHURCH STREET,
LONDON W8 7LP ✆ 020 7221 4026
Through the Looking Glass sells 19th-century and gilt mirrors. However, there are
other periods and styles as well as some paintings.

Mah's Antiques and Oriental Carpets 141 KENSINGTON CHURCH STREET,
LONDON W8 7LP ✆ 020 7229 9047
A large shop packed with all things 19th century European, including furniture,
ornate porcelain, oriental ceramics and works of art, Mah's is your quintessential
19th-century antique shop.

Patrick Sandberg Antiques 150–152 KENSINGTON CHURCH STREET,
LONDON W8 4BN ✆ 020 7229 0373 *www.antiquefurniture.net*
This gallery of fine English 18th- and early 19th-century antiques is beautifully presented
and particularly well known for large dining pieces. A Swedish business, Antik West,
also has its London showrooms within this shop, and the Chinese export and
Imperial porcelain complement the furniture for an all-out elegant look.

Butchoff Antiques 154 KENSINGTON CHURCH STREET, LONDON W8 4BN
✆ 020 7221 8174 *www.butchoff.com*
Ian Butchoff boasts a big, glamorous gallery presenting quality furniture and objects
from the mid-18th to the 19th century with flair. You can be sure of a warm welcome
and excellent humour as you peruse this Aladdin's cave.

Denton Antiques 156 KENSINGTON CHURCH STREET, LONDON W8 4BN
✆ 020 7229 5866 *www.denton-antiques.co.uk*
This opulent shop sells ornate European furniture, ormolu, cut glass and masses of
chandeliers. It is run by the same third-generation antique dealers as M. E. Crick (see
below). The two families married in the first half of the 20th century.

John Jesse 160 KENSINGTON CHURCH STREET,
LONDON W8 4BN ✆ 020 7229 0312
Keeping with the Kensington Church Street theme of high quality and specialization,
John Jesse sells 20th-century decorative arts, paintings and furniture.

Mrs M. E. Crick Chandeliers 166 KENSINGTON CHURCH STREET,
LONDON W8 4BN ✆ 020 7229 1338 *www.denton-antiques.co.uk*
Trading since 1900, this sumptuous shop specializes in chandeliers of all periods,
shapes and sizes. M. E. Crick also carries a large stock of wall lights, glass and ormolu
and is the place to buy replacement drops and faceted glass for lights.

Nassirzadeh Antiques 178 KENSINGTON CHURCH STREET,
LONDON W8 4DP ✆ 020 7243 8262
This old-fashioned antique shop sells all kinds of small valuables, including 19th-
century glass, porcelain, ormolu, oriental rugs and silver.

Sinai Antiques 219–221 KENSINGTON CHURCH STREET, LONDON W8 7LX ℂ 020 7229 6190

An opulent display of all things brilliant and grand, Sinai Antiques evokes the mood of an overflowing Edwardian country house with its stained glass, ormolu, gilt, orientalist antiques, sculpture and 19th-century furniture.

ORIENTAL SPECIALISTS

R. and G. McPherson Antiques 40 KENSINGTON CHURCH STREET, LONDON W8 4BX ℂ 020 7937 0812 *www.orientalceramics.com*

This first-generation oriental porcelain dealer has an obvious love and passion for his field. A wide range of periods and styles is displayed with accurate descriptions and reports on condition and authenticity. Unintimidating and friendly, this gallery sells oriental ceramics from ten to several thousand pounds, with a strength in Kangxi and blue and white.

Japanese Gallery 66D KENSINGTON CHURCH STREET, LONDON W8 4BY ℂ 020 7229 2934 *www.japanesegallery.co.uk*

A wide range of Japanese prints and works of art have been assembled here with true expertise. There is also a second branch at **Camden Passage (▶ 89)**.

Cohen & Cohen 101B KENSINGTON CHURCH STREET, LONDON W8 7LN ℂ 020 7727 7677 *www.cohenandcohen.co.uk*

A top-end dealer in the finest and rarest Chinese export porcelain, this shop is imbued with the grace of the oriental. A selection of decorative pieces acts as an accompaniment to the most unusual and highest-quality Chinese export. Cohen & Cohen travels throughout the world showing at various fairs.

Jorge Welsh Oriental Porcelain & Works of Art 116 KENSINGTON CHURCH STREET, LONDON W8 4BH ℂ 020 7229 2140 *www.jorgewelsh.com*

At this specialist shop, you will find Chinese porcelain from the Neolithic period to the Qing dynasty. Jorge Welsh is also one of the leading specialists in export for the Portuguese market and can be counted on to stock unusual and rare pieces.

Millner Manolatos 2 CAMPDEN STREET, LONDON W8 7EP ℂ 020 7229 3268 *www.arthurmillner.com*

Truly knowledgeable in this rarefied field, Indian and Islamic specialist Millner Manolatos offers a fascinating array of art and objects. The range includes bronzes, ivory, ceramics, textiles, paintings, books, prints and even jewelry and furniture, all presented with passion and expertise. Prices also range from a couple of hundred pounds to tens of thousands.

S. Marchant 120 KENSINGTON CHURCH STREET, LONDON W8 4BH ℂ 020 7229 5319 *www.marchantasianart.com*

This third-generation dealer sells the highest-quality Chinese and Japanese ceramics and works of art with specialities in Imperial, famille verte and the 16th and 17th centuries. Marchant has one of the best stocks in the world and a notable, genuine love of porcelain.

Amir Mohtashemi 131 KENSINGTON CHURCH STREET, LONDON W8 7LP
℗ 020 7727 2628 *www.amirmohtashemi.com*
Indian and Islamic works of art and furniture are the emphasis at this beautifully presented corner gallery. Pieces are of a high quality, and the interest in non-Western shapes and designs is like a breath of fresh air.

Geoffrey Waters 133 KENSINGTON CHURCH STREET, LONDON W8 7PL
℗ 020 7243 6081 *www.antique-chinese-porcelain.com*
Another dealer who has worked his way up through the ranks, Geoffrey Waters specializes in Chinese porcelain from the 16th to the 18th century. Strengths lie in the Kangxi blue and white and exportwares, and pieces are always honestly and accurately described.

J. A. N. Fine Art 134 KENSINGTON CHURCH STREET, LONDON W8 4BH
℗ 020 7792 0736 *www.jan-fineart-london.com*
The friendly gallery sells a pot-pourri of fine Chinese, Japanese and Korean porcelain and works of art with a wide range of prices.

Gregg Baker Asian Art 132 KENSINGTON CHURCH STREET, LONDON W8 4BN
℗ 020 7221 3533 *www.japanesescreens.com*
At Gregg Baker's you will find a beautiful, minimalist gallery specializing in antique Japanese screens. This dealer is truly a hidden gem, and those in the know call here for quality and fair prices.

Peter Kemp 170 KENSINGTON CHURCH STREET,
LONDON W8 4BN ℗ 020 7229 2988
Peter Kemp specializes in antique oriental and European porcelain and is a good trade call in these fields.

DEALERS IN CERAMICS AND GLASS

Mary Wise & Grosvenor Antiques 27 HOLLAND STREET,
LONDON W8 4NA ℗ 020 7937 8649 *www.wiseantiques.com*
An elegant and feminine shop, here you will find English, continental and oriental porcelain and works of art.

Jeanette Hayhurst Fine Glass 32A KENSINGTON CHURCH STREET,
LONDON W8 4HA ℗ 020 7938 1539
This wonderful glass gallery specializes in the finest British glass from the 17th to the 20th century.

E. and H. Manners 66A KENSINGTON CHURCH STREET, LONDON W8 4BY
℗ 020 7229 5516 *www.europeanporcelain.com*
Ex-**Christie's** specialists sell European ceramics and works of art of the finest quality.

Jonathan Horne 66C KENSINGTON CHURCH STREET, LONDON W8 4BY
℗ 020 7221 5658 *www.jonathanhorne.co.uk*
At this particularly English specialist gallery, you will find an amazing and large stock of some of the rarest and most collectible pieces of early English pottery. Jonathan

Horne boasts one of the largest stocks anywhere of English medieval pottery, early Delftware and Staffordshire, all pre-1830.

Garry Atkins 107 KENSINGTON CHURCH STREET, LONDON W8 7LN
℡ 020 7727 8737 *www.englishpottery.com*
The enthusiast and the general collector alike will love the charm, naiveté and rarity of this beautiful shop specializing in English 18th-century pottery.

Simon Spero 109 KENSINGTON CHURCH STREET,
LONDON W8 7LN ℡ 020 7727 7413
In a beautiful and charming shop, Simon Spero specializes in early English porcelain. He is also a published author on early Worcester and Bow porcelain and has written a price guide to English 18th-century porcelain.

Stockspring Antiques 114 KENSINGTON CHURCH STREET, LONDON W8 4BH
℡ 020 7727 7995 *www.antique-porcelain.co.uk*
This beautiful gallery sells fine English and continental 18th-century porcelain and organizes exhibitions on the same subjects as well as topics related to new discoveries and research in the porcelain field.

Roderick Jellicoe 3A CAMPDEN STREET, KENSINGTON CHURCH STREET,
LONDON W8 7EP ℡ 020 7727 1571 *www.englishporcelain.com*
You can buy here with confidence from one of the world experts in English 18th-century porcelain. Expect a warm welcome and clear enthusiasm while you choose from a selection that includes all the major 18th-century English factories.

Hope and Glory 131A KENSINGTON CHURCH STREET,
LONDON W8 7LP ℡ 020 7727 8424
Rows and rows of neatly displayed British commemorative ceramics and glass make Hope and Glory a collector's dream!

Libra Antiques 131D KENSINGTON CHURCH STREET,
LONDON W8 7LP ℡ 020 7727 2990
Libra Antiques is a must for the enthusiastic collector of English pottery, including earthenware and transferware.

WHERE TO EAT

Sally Clarke's 122 & 124 KENSINGTON CHURCH STREET, LONDON W8 4BH
℡ 020 7221 9225 *www.sallyclarke.com*
Sally Clarke's comprises a smart restaurant as well as a bakery and café with delicious and freshly made offerings.

The Churchill Arms 119 KENSINGTON CHURCH STREET,
LONDON W8 7LN ℡ 020 7727 4242
The Thai restaurant at the back of this charming, quirky Victorian pub is one of the best deals in ritzy Kensington and **Notting Hill**. The food is excellent and the friendly Irish publican may well come by to check on you and regale you with a story while you eat. Main courses cost around £6.

WHILE YOU'RE IN THE AREA

Kensington Palace KENSINGTON PALACE STATE APARTMENTS,
KENSINGTON GARDENS, LONDON W8 4PX © 0870 751 5170 *www.hrp.org.uk*
Originally a private country house, Kensington Palace was acquired in 1689 by King
William and Queen Mary and renovated by royal architect Sir Christopher Wren. The
palace was the birthplace and childhood home of Queen Victoria and was home to
Diana, Princess of Wales, up until her tragic death in 1997. Today the State Apart-
ments and the Royal Ceremonial Dress Collection, which includes dresses worn by
Queen Elizabeth II and Princess Diana, are open to the public. The palace is open
daily from 10 a.m. to 5 p.m., and until 6 p.m. during the summer season.

Leighton House 12 HOLLAND PARK ROAD, LONDON W14 8LZ
© 020 7602 3316 *www.rbkc.gov.uk/LeightonHouseMuseum*
The Victorian studio and home of Pre-Raphaelite artist Frederick, Lord Leighton,
Leighton House is a beautiful example of Victorian eclecticism and art. In addition to
the elaborate interior, the highlight of which is the Arab Hall with its Moorish tiles,
fountain and pool, there is an extremely good collection of art by Leighton and his
contemporaries. The house opens daily, except Tuesdays, from 11 a.m. until 5.30 p.m.

Kensington Church Street

NOTTING HILL

WESTBOURNE PARK TUBE STATION
(HAMMERSMITH + CITY LINE)

Westway (A40)

Portobello Road

Ledbury Road

LADBROKE GROVE
TUBE STATION
(HAMMERSMITH + CITY LINE)

Westbourne Grove

Pembridge Villas

Kensington Park Road

Pembridge Road

Ladbroke Road

Notting Hill Gate

Holland Park

NOTTING HILL GATE
TUBE STATION
(DISTRICT + CIRCLE
+ CENTRAL LINES)

WHAT'S THERE?

Portobello Road (with its eponymous market) and nearby streets make Notting Hill an antiques Mecca. In the 18th century, Portobello Road was a country lane connecting Notting Hill Gate to Portobello Farm, deriving its name from Admiral Vernon's capture of the Puerto Bello in the Caribbean. There are later descriptions of a market that lined the road in the 19th century, making it impassable to horse traffic, much as it is almost impassable to cars today.

Portobello Market developed into the antiques extravaganza that we know today after World War II, when 'rag and bone' men would gather to sell their wares. The market gained a reputation as a good place to buy antiques, especially for the knowledgeable dealer who could snap up bargains from sellers who might not know the true value of their wares.

Today, over 1500 dealers gather on a Saturday to sell from over thirty different markets and arcades as well as dozens of individual shops. The market has worldwide fame, drawing in thousands of professional dealers, private collectors and tourists alike on a weekly basis.

For the full experience, go on a Saturday morning when the street vendors, markets and arcades open from about 5 a.m. until mid-afternoon. If possible, try to be there before 10 a.m. when the real crowds start to arrive. Many shops are also open during the week, but a weekday visit will be a limited experience.

Although there is an element of Portobello Market that caters for tourists without much knowledge of antiques, the market is also a place where dealers go to buy and sell. There are often bargains to be had, and there is always a plethora of knowledgeable dealers from whom to learn.

WHEN IS IT OPEN?

Every Saturday the market begins at about 5 a.m., and it winds down in the early to mid afternoon. Various individual shops are also open during the week.

HOW TO GET THERE

By tube, go to Ladbroke Grove (Hammersmith & City line) station and turn immediately right as you come out of the station. This will put you at the end of the market that sells clothes, flowers, and fruit and vegetables. If you keep walking up Portobello Road, you will soon come to the antiques section.

Alternatively, from Notting Hill Gate (Central line) tube station, take the north exit out of the station and walk along Pembridge Road for a few moments until you see a roundabout. Stay on Pembridge Road, and the next road on the left will be the bottom end of Portobello Road.

By bus, you can take the 27 from Camden or Paddington, the 52 from Victoria or Hyde Park Corner, and the 70 from South Kensington (the same route that takes you to **Kensington Church Street**). Also, the 12 and 94 from either Piccadilly Circus or Oxford Circus, and the 148 from Victoria and Hyde Park Corner, will get you there.

HIGHLIGHTS

This is a fabulous place to buy at trade prices and is one of the few places in London where you can buy antiques for £100 or less. Because many dealers only sell from a stall in a market or arcade, they do not have the overheads of running a London shop and can pass on the savings to you. Many of London's high-end professional dealers come to Portobello early every Saturday to scour the market for fresh and sometimes under-valued goods.

LOWLIGHTS

Portobello Market can be extremely crowded, particularly in the late morning and early afternoon. The earlier you arrive, the more pleasant your experience will be. Also, beware of pickpockets.

WHERE TO GO

If you are looking for a specialist in a particular field, *www.portobelloroad.co.uk* is an excellent resource for locating dealers. From the homepage click on 'Specialist Dealer'.

As there are so many dealers from whom to choose, this section has been divided up into two categories: Saturday-only shops, arcades and markets, and shops and markets which are open all week.

SATURDAY-ONLY SHOPS, ARCADES AND MARKETS

Roger's Antique Gallery 65 PORTOBELLO ROAD, LONDON W11 2QB
This is a jewelry and silver arcade with ceramics, pipes and glass.

Chelsea Galleries, The Dealers' Gallery 67, 69 & 73 PORTOBELLO ROAD, LONDON W11 2QB
Befitting the market setting, a range of smart antiques is offered, including Chinese porcelain, ivory, instruments, jewelry, lighting and clocks.

Good Fairy Antique Market 100 PORTOBELLO ROAD, LONDON W11 2QD *www.goodfairyantiques.co.uk*
With antique jewelry, ceramics and silver, this is another typical Portobello market.

The Red Teapot Arcade 101/103 PORTOBELLO ROAD, LONDON W11 2QB
A particularly good range and quality of antiques can be found at the Red Teapot with varied offerings including faience, Delft, **Art Deco**, glass, silver, **Art Nouveau**, chinoiserie and some furniture. A particularly good individual dealer is Christophe Herren who has fine French and continental objects, lighting, Grand Tour pieces and some furniture.

Geoffrey Van Arcade 105/107 PORTOBELLO ROAD, LONDON W11 2QB
A good call if you are looking for a speciality item, this arcade has many collectible antiques such as tartanware, netsuke, corkscrews, Black Forrest carvings, papier mâché, chinoiserie and fans.

Antique Gallery 109 PORTOBELLO ROAD, LONDON W11 2QB
Visit this gallery for dealers specializing in prints, including maps from England and the rest of the world.

113 Portobello Road 113 PORTOBELLO ROAD, LONDON W11 2QB
A charming selection of antique ceramics, glass, lighting, prints, silver and jewelry can be found here.

115 Antiques 115 PORTOBELLO ROAD, LONDON W11 2DY
Number 155 houses three dealers selling 18th- and 19th-century boxes, glass and small silver, furniture and works of art.

117 117 PORTOBELLO ROAD, LONDON W11 2DY
Try this small venue for clocks and other instruments and objects.

Crown Arcade 119 PORTOBELLO ROAD, LONDON W11 2DY
Crown Arcade has a good range of small antiques, particularly antique boxes, glass, faience, Staffordshire, Chinese porcelain and **Arts & Crafts** objects.

The Silver Fox Gallery 121 PORTOBELLO ROAD, LONDON W11 2DY
The Silver Fox Gallery is a Saturday-only antique jewelry arcade.

Central Gallery 125 PORTOBELLO ROAD, LONDON W11 2DY
Antique jewelry is sold at this popular arcade.

Notting Hill

67

Admiral Vernon Antiques Market 141–149 PORTOBELLO ROAD, LONDON W11 2DY *www.portobello-antiques.co.uk*
Admiral Vernon's has many dealers offering a large range of antiques at an equally wide range of prices. You will find many things here to tempt you, including art glass, silver, textiles, Chinese porcelain and 18th-century objects, as well as an excellent seller of speciality antique and art books in the basement. If you need a few minutes to warm up and/or relax, have a drink at the in-house coffee shop.

Kleanthous Antiques 144 PORTOBELLO ROAD, LONDON W11 2DZ
© 020 7727 3649 *www.kleanthous.com*
A family-owned Portobello Road antique shop, Kleanthous sells traditional furniture, silver, works of art, jewelry and watches.

Delehar Antiques 146 PORTOBELLO ROAD, LONDON W11 2DZ © 020 7727 9860
This is a Saturday-only, old-fashioned antique shop, offering various genres and periods of antiques.

Dolphin Arcade 157 PORTOBELLO ROAD, LONDON W11 2DY
Dolphin Arcade has brass, hardware, Chinese porcelain, silver and British ceramics. Look hard for valuable pieces mixed in with general stock.

The Red Lion Antiques Arcade WORLDS FIRST, 165–169 PORTOBELLO ROAD, LONDON W11 2DY and
PORTWINE GALLERIES, 173/175 PORTOBELLO ROAD, LONDON W11 2DY
The dealers tend to be traders in the collectibles market at this end of Portobello Road, and at these two arcades the wares are piled high and require active searching on your part. Not for the faint-hearted or unenthusiastic!

Lipka's Antiques Gallery 282, 286, 288, 290 WESTBOURNE GROVE, LONDON W11 2PS
This is an enormous arcade with specialist dealers in a vast range of objects. On any particular Saturday, you might find watches, tribal art, jewelry, **rustic** and tramp art, prints, **Asian** objects and taxidermy.

287 and 289 287/289 WESTBOURNE GROVE, LONDON W11 2QA
Here you will find a good range of 19th-century furniture and porcelain, and a real strength in Chinese, Japanese and Indian ceramics and works of art.

20th Century Theatre 291 WESTBOURNE GROVE, LONDON W11 2QA
Connected to and thus part of 113 Portobello Road, a huge range of silver, books, ceramics, **Asian** decorative arts, European ceramics and kitchenalia is on offer with something for everyone.

293 293 WESTBOURNE GROVE, LONDON W11 2QA
At this typical Portobello market a range of objects such as Staffordshire, French ormolu and toys are sold with enthusiasm.

Burton Arcade 296 WESTBOURNE GROVE, LONDON W11 2PS
This is a small arcade with ceramics, clocks and 19th-century collectibles, including Staffordshire pottery and flatbacks.

Still Too Few 300 WESTBOURNE GROVE, LONDON W11 2PS
Go to Still Too Few for English country antiques. It offers kitchenalia, ginghams and some pine furniture.

SHOPS AND MARKETS OPEN ALL WEEK

75 Portobello Road 75 PORTOBELLO ROAD, LONDON W11 2QB
The phrase 'smart smalls' describes this shop, which houses four specialist dealers with separate businesses. Elizabeth Bradwin (*www.elizabethbradwin.com*) sells 19th- and 20th-century animal subjects, bronzes, Staffordshire, terracotta and tobacco jars. With his expert knowledge, Garrick Coleman (*www.antiquechess.co.uk*) has an amazing selection of the best chess sets available anywhere in the world. He also stocks antique paper weights. Gavin Douglas Fine Antiques (*www.antique-clocks.co.uk*) sells 18th- and 19th-century French and English clocks, porcelain and bronzes. Hickmet Fine Art (*www.hickmet.com*) sells 19th- and 20th-century European bronze, ivory and decorative glass.

Trude Weaver 71 PORTOBELLO ROAD, LONDON W11 2QB ✆ 020 7229 8738
This small shop has traditional English furniture and objects. With clean presentation and honest pieces, it feels like a friendly, provincial English antique dealer.

Portobello Antique Store 79 PORTOBELLO ROAD,
LONDON W11 2QB ✆ 020 7221 1994
If you are looking for the perfect antique silver pieces for the dinner table, you must call at this shop for a wide selection of cutlery, jugs, candlesticks and sparkling trays. It is closed on Sundays and Mondays.

Judy Fox 81 PORTOBELLO ROAD, LONDON W11 2QB ✆ 020 7229 8130
Fancy antiques, including 19th-century French and English pieces with inlay, ormolu and French polish, are accessorized with smaller objects such as collections of cut glass and walking sticks.

Barham Antiques 83 PORTOBELLO ROAD, LONDON W11 2QB
✆ 020 7727 3845 *www.barhamantiques.co.uk*
This is an old-fashioned antique shop, packed to the hilt with furniture, glass, brass, boxes and inkwells.

Alice's 86 PORTOBELLO ROAD, LONDON W11 2QD ✆ 020 7229 8187
Call at Alice's for a traditional English pub feel with lots of old and reproduction signs and canisters.

John Dale 87 PORTOBELLO ROAD, LONDON W11 2QB ✆ 020 7727 1304
John Dale deals in a range of small antiques, including glass, silver, small statues, prints and watercolours.

Atlam Silver 111 PORTOBELLO ROAD, LONDON W11 2QB
✆ 020 7602 7573 *www.atlamsilver.co.uk*
Atlam, a multi-dealer shop, has a very large selection of small antiques, including pill boxes, pocket watches, cachepots and picture frames.

Harris' Arcade 161/163 PORTOBELLO ROAD, LONDON W11 2DY
At the newly renovated Harris' Arcade you will find a range of dealers stocking silver, tribal art, prints, ceramics and glass as well as other, more unusual genres.

World Famous Portobello Market 177 PORTOBELLO ROAD, LONDON W11 2DY ℂ 020 7436 9416
Some shops in this arcade are open all week and cater for tourists. There is a range of antiques, including Russian and reproductions. A good dealer within the arcade is Justin F. Skrebowski Prints (*www.skreb.co.uk*) on the ground floor. There are thousands upon thousands of categorized prints. After a little bit of hunting, you can find something of interest to you or a unique present for someone else. The diverse subjects include architecture, science and geography, and the prices are modest considering the age.

M. C. N. Antiques 183 WESTBOURNE GROVE, LONDON W11 2SB ℂ 020 7727 3796
A gallery with an oriental focus, M. C. N. stocks Chinese and Japanese sculpture, screens and ceramics.

Jones Antique Lighting 194 WESTBOURNE GROVE, LONDON W11 2RH ℂ 020 7229 6866
A great selection of early 20th-century **Art Nouveau** and **Art Deco** lighting (including hanging ceiling pieces and sconces) is sold at this packed lighting shop.

Lacy Gallery 203 WESTBOURNE GROVE, LONDON W11 2SB ℂ 020 7229 6340
Lacy Gallery is the one-call stop for antique picture frames of all periods, styles and prices.

Arbras Gallery 292 WESTBOURNE GROVE, LONDON W11 2PS ℂ 020 7229 6772
This arcade sells silver as well as other small, general antiques.

The Westbourne Print & Map Shop 297 WESTBOURNE GROVE, LONDON W11 2QA ℂ 020 7792 9673
The prints and maps here are all well organized by period and subject, and the friendly dealer has very amenable opening hours from Tuesday to Saturday inclusive.

Cura Antiques 34 LEDBURY ROAD, LONDON W11 2AB ℂ 020 7229 6880 *www.cura-antiques.com*
With a mixture of the best Italian furniture and paintings from the 16th to the early 19th century, Cura feels like a traditional continental antiques gallery. From the *kunstkammer* (cabinet of curiosities) to the Grand Tour, here you will experience the world of the aristocratic collector.

Robin Martin Antiques 44 LEDBURY ROAD, LONDON W11 2AB ℂ 020 7727 1301
This smart shop is home to a second-generation antique dealer with fine English as well as high-quality, quirky pieces from all corners of the Empire. The owner, Paul, has a fresh approach to antiques with a keen eye for rare and unusual pieces. In a traditional setting you might find a Chippendale chest with Chinese porcelain, set next to a 1920s mirror under a 1930s chandelier. The pieces are united by a relaxed elegance and good quality throughout.

B & T Antiques 47 LEDBURY ROAD, LONDON W11 2AG
℘ 020 7229 7001 *www.bntantiques.co.uk*
For a slightly more modern feel, try B & T Antiques with its mirrored, glamorous **Art Deco** furniture and lighting with that stylish, seductive French *je ne sais quoi.*

Michael Davidson 54 LEDBURY ROAD, LONDON W11 2AJ ℘ 020 7229 6088
Expect traditional continental and English furniture and objects.

F. E. A. Briggs 77 LEDBURY ROAD, LONDON W11 2AG ℘ 020 7727 0909
For a taste of what antique dealers and furniture restorers of Notting Hill used to be like before the cool coffee shops and posh clothes boutiques moved in, step into F. E. A. Briggs. Here you will find an old-fashioned antique shop with traditional English brown furniture.

M. & D. Lewis 1 LONSDALE ROAD, LONDON W11 2BY ℘ 020 7727 3908
Here you will find a pleasant array of traditional English and continental antiques, including furniture (decorated with giltwood and marquetry), mirrors, porcelain and works of art, and most pieces are from the 19th century.

Sebastiano Barbagallo 15–17 PEMBRIDGE ROAD, LONDON W11 3HG ℘ 020 7792 3320
Asian, tribal, Communist and Maoist artefacts make an eclectic mix of all things Eastern from the past two thousand years.

Jack Casimir 23 PEMBRIDGE ROAD, LONDON W11 3HG ℘ 020 7727 8643
This BADA and LAPADA dealer sells all things brass and metal. Visit for your perfect pair of candlesticks, a bedwarmer or fire screen to evoke the 18th-century mood at home.

Hirst Antiques 59 PEMBRIDGE ROAD, LONDON W11 3HG ℘ 020 7727 9364
Furniture, prints, chandeliers, textiles, jewelry, sconces, statues, relics and bric-a-brac are piled high at this old-fashioned shop. This is grandma's attic done with vintage style and flair.

Mercury Antiques 1 LADBROKE ROAD, LONDON W11 3PA ℘ 020 7727 5106
This tidy, pretty gallery displaying British ceramics is located close to Notting Hill tube station. Don't be fooled into thinking that this is a knick-knack shop. Mercury is a well-organized and presented gallery of 18th- and early 19th-century English porcelain, pottery and glass. The perfect labelling attests to the expertise of this dealer.

WHERE TO EAT

Osteria Basilico 29 KENSINGTON PARK ROAD, LONDON W11 2EU ℘ 020 7727 9372
You will find this Tucson-styled eatery just off Portobello Road. It can be crowded, but the number of locals assures you of the quality and popularity of the freshly prepared Italian dishes.

Cafe 206 206 WESTBOURNE GROVE,
LONDON W11 2RH *©* 020 7221 1535
At this simple and inexpensive café you will find sandwiches, Brazilian fare and coffee.
During good weather, there are plenty of tables on the pavement for you to sit outside
and watch the world go by.

WHILE YOU'RE IN THE AREA

Holland Park THE STABLE YARD, W8 6LU *©* 020 7602 2226
Head to Holland Park (entrances on Abbotsbury Road, Holland Park, Holland Walk
and Kensington High Street) to get away from crowds and noise. The park includes a
beautiful and peaceful Japanese Garden as well as a gorgeous Jacobean house built
for James I's Chancellor of the Exchequer in 1607, which is now used as a Youth
Hostel. There is a café for refreshments where you can relax, watch peacocks and sift
through your purchases.

Electric Cinema 191 PORTOBELLO ROAD, LONDON W11 2ED
© 020 7908 9696 *www.electriccinema.co.uk*
Although one of the last buildings to be built on Portobello Road, the Electric Cinema
was one of the first buildings on Portobello Road to have electricity – hence the name.
An old advertisement for the Electric Cinema states, 'afternoon teas served in all parts
[of the auditorium] and reserved fauteuils at 1s'. Tickets may now be more expensive,
but you can still view films in period splendour and comfort since the cinema's refurbishment and reopening in 2001.

Eclectic

CHURCH STREET MARYLEBONE

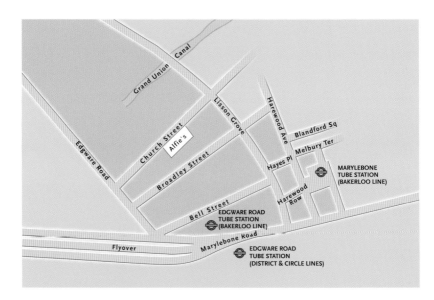

WHAT'S THERE?

Church Street, although only three quarters of a mile from Marble Arch (at the western end of Oxford Street), is London's lost antique district. There has been a market on Church Street since the 1830s when it only sold produce. It became an antiques destination in 1976 when Alfie's Antique Market took over the old Jordan's department store. After 1988's extensive refurbishment, Alfie's now spans 35,000 square feet, making it London's largest indoor antique market.

Alfie's maintains a funky edge, and it is telling that its website shows the greatest number of dealers specializing in **Art Deco**, **Art Nouveau** and decorative arts along with glass and ceramics. On the ground floor, Sparkle Moore's homage to the 1950s ranges from fabulous fashions to battery-operated hula-girl shakers, and although not strictly antique, Sparkle's store is compulsory viewing.

Over the years, about twenty antique shops have sprouted up along Church Street and around the corner (towards the Sea Shell Restaurant) on Lisson Grove. Some are Alfie's 'graduates', others have just been attracted to the area. These shops are a staple trade call – a place that dealers go to in order to buy. Church Street offers a mix of traditional brown and decorative antiques in a mid-market price range.

WHEN IS IT OPEN?

As Alfie's hours are 10 a.m. to 6 p.m. Tuesday to Saturday, the other shops on the street tend to follow suit. You may find that fewer individual shops open on a Saturday.

HOW TO GET THERE

The best underground station for Church Street is Marylebone (Bakerloo line). As you come out of the station on to Harewood Avenue, turn right, and make a quick left on to Hays Place. Turn right on to the first crossroads which is Lisson Grove. Walk along Lisson Grove, past the Sea Shell Restaurant (on your left), and then the next street on your left will be Church Street.

By bus, the 6 and 98 from Oxford Circus, the 414 from South Kensington, and the 16 from Hyde Park Corner take you to the bottom of Church Street and Edgware Road where you will need to walk up past the Church Street Market to get to the antique shops. Alternatively, the 139 and 189 from Oxford Circus take you to Lisson Grove where it meets Church Street and thus requires less walking.

HIGHLIGHTS

The boys at Horneman Antiques are fabulous (Preston Fitzgerald is a separate dealer upstairs). Horneman stocks beautiful French and northern European pieces, while Fitzgerald – a blond Jerry Seinfeld among other talents – single-handedly revives the Grand Tour.

LOWLIGHTS

The non-antiques end of Church Street is not one of London's most attractive areas!

WHERE TO GO

Gallery of Antique Costume and Textiles 2 CHURCH STREET, LONDON NW8 8ED ✆ 020 7723 9981 *www.gact.co.uk*
This is a must-see gallery for anyone at all interested in antique textiles and costume. In addition to antique wall hangings from the Middle East, China and Europe, experience the magic of period costumes, antique curtains and a range of opulent cushions made from Aubusson, tapestry and silk brocades. Movie directors, actors and models can sometimes be seen scouring the stock for the perfect, rare costume.

Magus 4 CHURCH STREET, LONDON NW8 8ED ✆ 020 7724 1278
Magus's decorative look comprises **painted** 19th-century **French** furniture, **folk art**, late 19th- and early 20th-century lighting and 1920s and 30s pieces.

Davidson Antiques 5 CHURCH STREET, LONDON NW8 8EE
✆ 020 7724 7781 *www.davidsonandmorgan.com*
Davidson's has a wide range of elegant and formal furniture and objects, ormolu, and detailed inlay from period to modern, with a real emphasis on glamour.

Tara 6 CHURCH STREET, LONDON NW8 8ED ✆ 020 7724 2405
This fabulous, packed antique shop sells furniture and objects to suit all tastes and budgets. With a speciality in all that is quirky, **rustic** and unusual, banjo-playing Irish dealer Gerry will keep you looking through literally thousands of pieces for your perfect treasure.

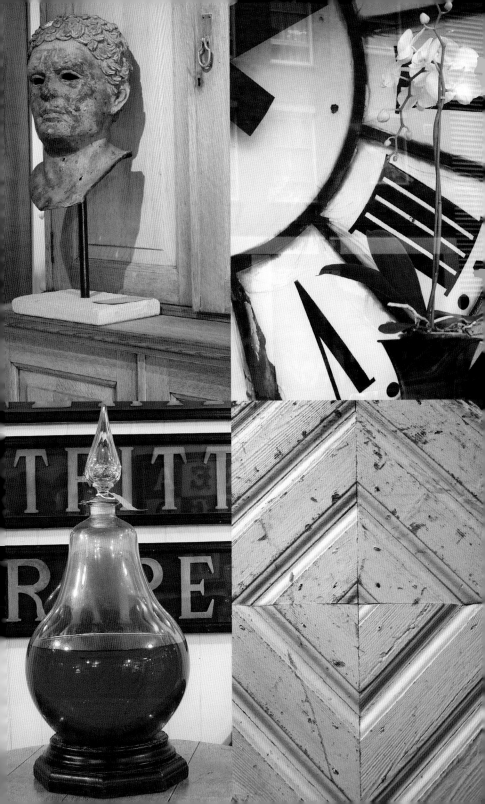

Church Street Antiques 8 CHURCH STREET,
LONDON NW8 8ED *©* 020 7723 7415
This shop sells mostly 19th- and early 20th-century antiques, many in revivalist styles, and often decorated with ormolu or inlay. There is a sense of the Edwardian fancy here and a range of hanging metal ceiling lights.

Nick Haywood 9 CHURCH STREET, LONDON NW8 8EE *©* 020 7224 9629
One of the new breed of 'antique' dealers, Haywood encourages the collecting of modern pieces. His store is made up of fewer antiques and more vintage pieces, particularly lighting and furniture from the 1920s to the 1970s.

Horneman Antiques 11 CHURCH STREET, LONDON NW8 8EE
© 020 7724 0404 *www.hornemanantiques.com*
An elegant gallery, Horneman Antiques resonates with grace and sells all things beautiful and charming. Raymond's stock includes French 18th-century furniture and objects of art, English early 19th-century antiques, old master drawings and Chinese and Japanese porcelain. Upon entering you will feel as though you have come into a tasteful, continental drawing room rather than an antiques gallery.

Preston Fitzgerald Antiques UPSTAIRS AT 11 CHURCH STREET, LONDON NW8 8EE
© 07734 053 625 *www.pfantiques.com*
Above Horneman, Preston's salon is an ode to the Neo-Classical. This specialist dealer has all things in the 19th-century Neo-Classical taste with a Greek and Roman flavour. Both novice and connoisseur will be tempted by formal English and continental mahogany furniture, Grand Tour objects, including plaques and intaglios, and thousands of prints. Preston's expertise, speciality and enthusiasm are clearly exemplified by his collection of English Greek and Roman revival ceramics, which is possibly the largest collection in the world of its type. Also keeping with the Grand Tour theme is an extensive selection of objects and art from all corners of the Empire, Islamic, Anglo-Indian and even Assyrian. From £10 to £10,000, prices are competitive, and the jokes come free.

Young & Son 12 CHURCH STREET, LONDON NW8 8EP
© 020 7723 5910 *www.youngandson.com*
This Church Street dealer has a wide range of styles and types of antiques with a particular strength in late 19th- and early 20th-century furniture, objects and art. On any particular day, you might find an aesthetic period table and oriental ceramics, as well as a large selection of paintings and drawings. Leon's wide range of stock has a quick turnaround, so it is always worth calling at this shop.

Alfie's Antique Market 13–25 CHURCH STREET, LONDON NW8 8DT
© 020 7723 6066 *www.alfiesantiques.com*
The range of antiques sold by more than one hundred individual dealers includes **Art Deco**, silver, furniture, paintings, prints, jewelry, ceramics, textiles and vintage clothing. Alfie's is developing into a great centre for **mid-century modern** design, particularly dealers Monica Glerean and Vincenzo Caffarella (*www.vinca.co.uk*), although there are still many dealers in traditional 18th- and 19th-century antiques. The particularly low overheads at Alfie's mean that prices tend to be competitive. Regardless of your taste and budget, you can easily spend an hour or more strolling along Alfie's corridors.

Marchand 14 CHURCH STREET, LONDON NW8 8EP ⓒ 020 7724 9238
Refined and eclectic, Marchand has antiques of many periods and styles from the
18th century to early 20th-century modernism. Expect to find furniture, Venetian
mirrors, French posters and all things subtle and sophisticated.

Gallery 1930 18 CHURCH STREET, LONDON NW8 8EP
ⓒ 020 7723 1555 *www.susiecooperceramics.com*
This shop specializes in both furniture and decorative arts from the 1920s and 30s,
with a particular emphasis on ceramics – including Susie Cooper, Keith Murray,
Clarice Cliff and Lalique. Call here for all your **Art Deco** and 1930s modernism needs.

Just Desks 20 CHURCH STREET, LONDON NW8 8EP ⓒ 020 7723 7976
This store has a huge selection of old and new traditional desks.

Bloch Antiques 22 CHURCH STREET, LONDON NW8 8EP ⓒ 020 7723 6575
This **new school** dealer on Church Street has an appealing and well-presented shop.
The bold antique furniture is decorative without being fussy. You will find pieces from
18th-century country to 20th-century **Arts & Crafts** mixed in with architectural objects.

Bizarre 24 CHURCH STREET, LONDON NW8 8EP
ⓒ 020 7724 1305 *www.antiques-uk.co.uk/bizarre*
A fabulous call for the highest-quality, opulent **Art Deco** furniture, Bizarre commands
attention. You will feel like you have stepped back into a luxurious 1920s apartment.

Cristobal 26 CHURCH STREET, LONDON NW8 8EP
ⓒ 020 7724 7230 *www.cristobal.co.uk*
This feminine and glamorous shop sells 19th- and early 20th-century decorative
furniture, objects, chandeliers, mirrors and costume jewelry, all with pretty style.

Beverly 30 CHURCH STREET, LONDON NW8 8EP ⓒ 020 7262 1576
Packed with 1920s and 1930s ceramics, Beverly specializes in tea cups and saucers.

Jazzy Art Deco 34 CHURCH STREET, LONDON NW8 8EP
ⓒ 020 7724 0837 *www.jazzyartdeco.com*
This **Art Deco** specialist is the place to go for the rare blonde woods of Art Deco, such
as sycamore, maple and satinwood. Jazzy Art Deco stocks some of the best Art Deco
in London including complete suites.

Andrew Nebbett Antiques 35–37 CHURCH STREET, LONDON NW8 8ES
ⓒ 020 7723 2303 *www.andrewnebbett.com*
Ranging in period and style from 1750 to 1950, the furniture here is generally selected for
its clean and simple designs. By mixing in a few objects that are not ordinarily sold as
antiques, such as a utilitarian haberdasher's cabinet or a saddle rack, Andrew Nebbett
creates an eclectic and decorative look which is surprisingly modern.

North West Eight 36 CHURCH STREET, LONDON NW8 8EP ⓒ 020 7723 9337
At NW8 several dealers mix and display decorative and colourful antiques. Most
pieces are continental 19th and 20th century with **painted** furniture, gardenalia and
pretty mirrors. This is the perfect place for your **shabby chic** or slightly **folksy** look.

Raffles 40 CHURCH STREET, LONDON NW8 8EP ℂ 020 7724 6384

Raffles is an old-fashioned antique shop with interesting furniture and objects. There are no signs of minimalism or modernism in this shop. Charming and friendly Marilyn will be happy to show you Chinese porcelain, Anglo-Indian, **folk art** and traditional English pieces which are sourced by connoisseur dealer David. This is a wonderful fantasia of decorative and unusual items which do more than follow the trends in interior design.

Patricia Harvey Antiques and Decoration 42 CHURCH STREET, LONDON NW8 8EP ℂ 020 7262 8989 *www.patriciaharveyantiques.co.uk*

This is one of the best decorative antique shops in London. Pieces are selected for their beauty, charm and interest and include **painted** furniture, feminine French accessories, animal subjects and garden decoration. Patricia stocks antiques for decorating your home and making it a comfortable and engaging setting.

Victoria Harvey at Deuxieme 44 CHURCH STREET, LONDON NW8 8EP ℂ 020 7724 0738

Daughter of Patricia Harvey, Victoria's look is similar with **painted** 19th-century **French** and English furniture. Victoria also shrewdly mixes in 20th-century items, including **Art Deco**, 1930s modernism and even **rustic** and architectural pieces, to give an informal and soft look.

Madeline Crispin 95 LISSON GROVE, LONDON NW1 6UP ℂ 020 7402 6845

Selling quality antiques, mostly English 18th and 19th century, this shop is the place to go if your budget is a little bigger and you are looking for the more serious, brown piece.

The Façade 99 LISSON GROVE, LONDON NW1 6UP ℂ 020 7258 2017 *www.thefacade.co.uk*

This specialist lighting shop has an abundance of early 20th-century French and Italian chandeliers, sconces and lamps.

WHERE TO EAT

Roof Top Restaurant 13–25 CHURCH STREET, LONDON NW8 8DT

Church Street commands a few hours of even the speediest shopper's time, so a break is essential. Ex-New Yorker, Renaissance man and Church Street dealer Preston Fitzgerald is also a graduate of London's Le Cordon Bleu cooking school. He recommends the Roof Top Restaurant at Alfie's. 'It's more of a café than a restaurant, but for a light bite after antiquing, the Roof Top is a hidden gem. Try to find a seat outside on a warm day,' he says. 'Alternatively, if you must try English fish and chips, London's best may be found at the Sea Shell Restaurant about 100 yards/90 metres to the right at 49–51 Lisson Grove.'

Cali Café 39 CHURCH STREET, LONDON NW8 8ES ℂ 020 7262 5944

For Italian sandwiches and deli food, try this informal and bustling Latin American café. You will be able to sit outside and watch who goes in and out of the antique shops on Church Street. This is the perfect place for a quick, refreshing stop.

WHILE YOU'RE IN THE AREA

Camden Lock – On Foot

If you don't mind walking and the weather is fine, walk north on Lisson Grove over the canal and take the first right on the path down to the Grand Union Canal. From here you can walk along the canal through Regent's Park (and through the centre of London Zoo inside the Park) to Camden Lock. On weekends, one of London's largest markets (not antiques) takes place at Camden Lock. This attracts tens if not hundreds of thousands of people, so be prepared.

Camden Lock – By Boat

If you do mind walking and the weather is fine, take a short cab ride to 'Jason's Trip' at the intersection of Clifton Villas and Blomfield Road. Take a canal boat ride to Camden Lock. (Check times and availability at *www.jasons.co.uk* or ℂ 020 7286 3428.)

Abbey Road

If you're a Beatles fan, turn left on Lisson Grove which soon becomes Abbey Road. The studios of the same name are about half a mile ahead at the intersection with Grove End Road.

Lord's Cricket Ground   ST JOHN'S WOOD ROAD, LONDON NW8 8QN
ℂ 020 7616 8500 *www.lords.org*

'The Ashes' are the closest thing the game of cricket has to a relic. They are kept in a tiny urn which Australia and England compete for every other year. Curiously the Ashes are kept at Lord's Cricket Ground despite Australia 'winning' them every time since anyone can remember. To see the Ashes, turn left at Lisson Grove, then right at the first set of traffic lights on to St John's Wood Road. Lord's Cricket Ground and its museum will then be on your left.

Quirky
CAMDEN PASSAGE ISLINGTON

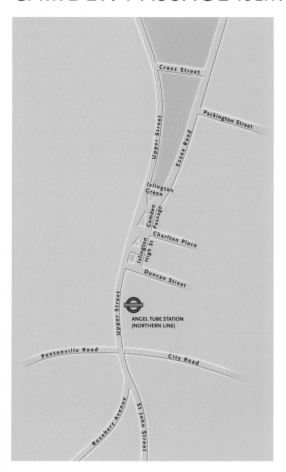

WHAT'S THERE?

Camden Passage is located in London's fashionable Islington, rather than in Camden, as the name suggests. Back in the 1700s, Islington – to the north of London's medieval centre – was a country village and a favourite retreat for well-to-do city-dwellers, including diarist Samuel Pepys. The Angel Inn at the crossroads of City Road and Upper Street, which unfortunately no longer stands but is commemorated by a plaque, was featured in Charles Dickens's *Oliver Twist*.

Going to Camden Passage is like stepping back in time. Created in 1766, it was a regular haunt of poet Charles Lamb, who lived in a cottage just around the corner. Although bombed during World War II, Camden Passage has retained most of its former charm. The first antique market was opened in the early 1960s, and it has since become a world-renowned antiques centre, offering something for everyone –

Camden Passage

fine silver, art, porcelain, jewelry and glassware. It has a good mix of permanent shops, multi-dealer malls, covered stands and people laying out knick-knacks on the pavement. Expect to find decorative antiques here with stock generally priced between a few hundred and a few thousand pounds.

As there are technically over 300 dealers in Camden Passage, this section divides the dealers into two groups:

• **Arcades and Markets** – smaller dealers

• **Shops** – the larger dealers with independent shops

WHEN IS IT OPEN?

Although some of the shops have longer hours, Camden Passage is in full swing on Wednesdays from 7 a.m. to 3 p.m., and Saturdays from 8 a.m. until 4 p.m. Occasionally, dealers will close earlier if the weather is particularly good or bad.

HOW TO GET THERE

Take the Northern line (Bank branch) to Angel tube station. As you come up what is reputably the longest escalator in Europe at Angel station, you are on the correct side of Upper Street and pointing directly towards Camden Passage. Exit the station and you will find the antiques area 100 yards/90 metres ahead of you, set slightly to the right of Upper Street. Angel Islington is very well connected. A number of buses pass along Upper Street or very close to Upper Street. The following list will show you some of the buses you could catch: 4, 19, 20, 38, 43, 56, 73, 153, 205, 214, 274, 341 and 476.

HIGHLIGHTS

The vast range of mid-market decorative items and the many trendy restaurants and cafés make for a thoroughly enjoyable day.

LOWLIGHTS

None spring to mind except a marked lack of public WC facilities.

WHERE TO GO

ARCADES AND MARKETS

These malls and arcades tend to house small dealers who prefer being open only two days a week. Their establishments are sometimes modest, but you will often find excellent value and, at times, unrivalled specialist knowledge.

The Mall Arcade 359 UPPER STREET, LONDON N1 OPD
This distinctive, long building has a special appeal with individual shops selling furniture downstairs and small, smart antiques on the ground floor, including silver, clocks, **Arts & Crafts**, jewelry and ceramics.

Gateway Arcade CAMDEN PASSAGE, LONDON N1 OPD

The dealers set their wares out on tables at this indoor market which boasts a variety of jewelry, militaria, prints and collectibles.

Angel Arcade 118 ISLINGTON HIGH STREET, LONDON N1 8EG

Inside this arcade you will find a range of **rustic**, tramp and **folk art**, courtesy of Kate Bannister and Austin-Cooper. Elegant chandeliers, Venetian mirrors and French 19th-century furniture are at the back with Maureen Lyons. Angel Arcade also houses a 20th-century lighting specialist, a dealer in doll furniture and several other dealers with an ever-changing stock of decorative antiques.

Pierrepont Arcade CAMDEN PASSAGE, LONDON N1 8EF

This arcade has a small covered area, where stallholders display their wares on tables, and a U-shaped parade of shops. Jubilee specializes in gorgeous 19th-century photographs, K. R. Goddard in prints, and Chris Tapsey in brown furniture and Chinese and Japanese ceramics. You will also find a wide selection of 18th- and 19th-century ceramics (including Quimper) at Caroline Carrier's and other dealers in an array of fields, including toys, silver, watches, jewelry and fountain pens. Interestingly, Pierrepont Arcade was built after a World War II bomb levelled its predecessor.

Fleamarket Arcade 7 PIERREPONT ROW, CAMDEN PASSAGE, LONDON N1 8EE

Tucked away behind Charlton Place and Camden Passage and at the back of Pierrepont Arcade, this arcade offers a selection of silver and prints.

The Georgian Village Antique Centre 30–31 ISLINGTON GREEN, LONDON N1 8DU

This arcade has a variety of small shops with dealers who are specialists in a chosen niche. Each offers choice and quality in their particular area of expertise. There are dealers in **Art Deco**, jewelry, 20th-century memorabilia, silver, tiles, collectibles, kitchenalia and an excellent selection of fine antique glass on the first floor. The annexed shops are specialists in **Art Nouveau**, continental 19th-century porcelain and toys. Chris Newland (in the basement) stocks traditional English furniture and works of art.

The Open Markets

Dealers set out their wares on tables and blankets, and stock varies greatly from week to week but usually includes jewelry, brass, collectibles and other general items.

SHOPS

Max-Oliver 108 ISLINGTON HIGH STREET, LONDON N1 8EG
℗ 020 7354 0777 *www.max-oliver.co.uk*

A newcomer to Camden Passage, Max-Oliver has a definite feminine air with vintage French furniture, chandeliers, mirrors and textiles.

Out Of The Attic / Fuori dalla Soffitta 112 ISLINGTON HIGH STREET, LONDON N1 8EG ℗ 020 7359 1213

The charming Italian proprietors sell decorative French and Italian silver, chandeliers, **painted** furniture and **rustic** ceramics, all with panache. Call here for a wide selection of antiques and a guaranteed friendly reception.

Vincent Freeman 1 CAMDEN PASSAGE, LONDON N1 8EA
℡ 020 7226 6178 *www.vincentfreemanantiques.com*
A quirky Camden passage specialist, Freeman is your call for a great selection of
19th-century music boxes and antique furniture.

Agnes Wilton 3 CAMDEN PASSAGE, LONDON N1 8ED ℡ 020 7226 5679
Here you will find mostly 19th- and 20th-century English furniture and objects including
Staffordshire flatbacks.

Christopher House Antique Trader 5B CAMDEN PASSAGE,
LONDON N1 8EA ℡ 020 7354 3603
A traditional English and continental furniture dealer with pieces from the 17th to the
20th century, Christopher House also sells **Asian** objects and more decorative pieces.

Mike Weedon 7 CAMDEN PASSAGE, LONDON N1 8EA
℡ 020 7226 5319 *www.mikeweedonantiques.com*
Step back in time with this excellent **Art Nouveau** and **Art Deco** dealer.

John Laurie Antiques 352 UPPER STREET, LONDON N1 0PD ℡ 020 7226 0913
Visit John Laurie to satiate your silver and plate needs and desires.

Tempus Antiques 13 CAMDEN PASSAGE, LONDON N1 8EA
℡ 020 7359 9555 *www.tempusantiques.com*
A fantasia of rich and lavish clocks, ormolu, objects and French 19th-century furniture
tempt those with a need for glamour in their lives.

Vane House Antiques 15 CAMDEN PASSAGE,
LONDON N1 8EA ℡ 020 7359 1343
For the traditionalist, Vane House offers a large supply of high-quality English 18th-
and 19th-century furniture.

Kevin Page Oriental Art 2–6 CAMDEN PASSAGE, LONDON N1 8ED
℡ 020 7226 8558 *www.kevinpage.co.uk*
With clarity of vision and an absolutely enormous stock of Chinese, Japanese and Korean
ceramics and works of art, Kevin Page is a treasure chest for collectors and designers
alike. Pieces are displayed opulently, and Japanese works of art are a particular strength.

David Griffith Antiques 17 CAMDEN PASSAGE,
LONDON N1 8EA ℡ 020 7226 1126
This bold, sumptuous shop stocks traditional, mostly 19th-century English antiques,
with a clubby feel. David also sells antique shop fittings and period office furniture.

Charlton House Antiques 19 CAMDEN PASSAGE,
LONDON N1 8EA ℡ 020 7226 3141
Bedecked with dazzling and lavish 19th- and early 20th-century furniture, convex mirrors
and chandeliers, Charlton House offers sparkle and glamour to brighten up any interior.

Diana Huntley 8 CAMDEN PASSAGE, LONDON N1 8ED ℡ 020 7226 4605
A specialist porcelain dealer with 19th-century continental and English factories, Diane
Huntley has the rare pieces required to crown any general collection.

Style Gallery 10 CAMDEN PASSAGE, LONDON N1 8ED
© 020 7359 7867 *www.styleantiques.co.uk*
A true Camden Passage gem, Style Gallery stocks a selection of striking and carefully chosen **Art Nouveau** and **Art Deco** furniture and works of art, all of the highest quality and epitomizing the era.

Japanese Gallery 23 CAMDEN PASSAGE, LONDON N1 8EA
© 020 7226 3347 *www.japanesegallery.co.uk*
This gallery focuses on the many art forms from Japan, with a particular strength in the prints and design which influenced late 19th-century Western arts. A second location on **Kensington Church Street** offers the same genres (▶ 60).

Origin 25 CAMDEN PASSAGE, LONDON N1 8EA
© 020 7704 1326 *www.origin101.co.uk*
Origin is a 20th-century modernism specialist with many Scandinavian pieces, and is a one shop stop for definitive **mid-century modern** designs.

Rosemary Conquest 27 CAMDEN PASSAGE, LONDON N1 8EA
© 020 7359 0616 *www.rosemaryconquest.com*
Rosemary Conquest is one of London's foremost purveyors of **painted French** decorative furniture and chandeliers. A sense of whimsy is evident with fairground, garden and animal decorations.

Tadema Gallery 10 CHARLTON PLACE, LONDON N1 8AJ
© 020 7359 1055 *www.tademagallery.com*
Jewelry crosses the line into art at Tadema, which has one of the best collections of **Arts & Crafts**, **Art Nouveau** and **Art Deco** jewelry.

Cloud Cuckoo Land 6 CHARLTON PLACE, LONDON N1 8AJ © 020 7354 3141
A popular haunt of vintage clothing enthusiasts, this is a Camden Passage trademark, easily identified by the tulle dress hanging outside above the shop sign.

Annie's Antique Clothes 12 CAMDEN PASSAGE,
LONDON N1 8ED © 020 7359 0796
Visit Annie's, another vintage clothing and textile specialist, for the quintessential 30s and 40s look.

Piers Rankin 14 CAMDEN PASSAGE, LONDON N1 8ED
© 020 7354 3349 *www.antiqueslondon.co.uk*
Highly ornate and decorative candlesticks, centrepieces and animal objects are offered at this antique silver and silver plate dealer.

Carlton Davidson 33 CAMDEN PASSAGE, LONDON N1 8EA © 020 7226 7491
With flamboyant style, Carlton Davidson stocks antique lighting and French furniture.

Vintage 18 18 CAMDEN PASSAGE, LONDON N1 8EA © 020 7359 6541
Selling a mix of furniture, which may include traditional English country furniture and some 20th-century items, you never know what you may find here, and Chris Paraskova has a range of the weird and wonderful.

Camden Passage

Gordon Gridley Antiques 41 CAMDEN PASSAGE,
LONDON N1 8ED ℗ 020 7226 0643
Folk art charm abounds at Gordon Gridley with quirky English and French pieces. Expect the unexpected with interesting furniture, naive art, doll's houses for the girls and ship models for the boys.

Sek Met Galleries 47 CAMDEN PASSAGE, LONDON N1 8EA ℗ 020 7354 2308
At this small shop with paintings, porcelain and jewelry, you will find inspiration to create an ornate and fancy boudoir look.

A and L Wax 49 CAMDEN PASSAGE, LONDON N1 8EA ℗ 020 7288 1939
A beautiful selection of silver trays, tea services and champagne buckets awaits at A and L Wax. There are also other pieces for the table in **Art Nouveau** and elegant, classic styles.

David Loveday, Furniture Vault 50 CAMDEN PASSAGE,
LONDON N1 8EA ℗ 020 7354 1047
This is the north London branch of David Loveday (the other is on **King's Road**), with high-quality English 18th- and 19th-century traditional brown furniture. The bold look is softened with decorative objects.

York Gallery 51 CAMDEN PASSAGE, LONDON N1 8EA
℗ 020 7354 8012 *www.yorkgallery.co.uk*
At York Gallery there are antique prints of all kinds, framed and presented in a friendly and approachable atmosphere.

Jonathan James 52–53 CAMDEN PASSAGE,
LONDON N1 8EA ℗ 020 7704 8266
At this three-storey shop of English furniture, you will find consistently good quality, which is well presented and brightened with brass and ceramics. Exploring this venue is a delight.

WHERE TO EAT

Trattoria Aquilino 31 CAMDEN PASSAGE, LONDON N1 8EA ℗ 020 7704 8593
Right in Camden Passage and nestled between the antique shops, this traditional trattoria with tasty Italian fare is perfect for lunch when you do not wish to miss a beat.

The Elk in the Woods 39 CAMDEN PASSAGE,
LONDON N1 8EA ℗ 020 7226 3535
This laid-back Islington eatery is also in the centre of Camden Passage. Serving hot sandwiches, chips and cooked meals, The Elk in the Woods is a cool place to relax and watch the comings and goings. In good weather, try to get a table outdoors.

Tinderbox Coffee Shop 21 UPPER STREET, LONDON N1 0PQ ℗ 020 7354 8929
You may enjoy joining the local, liberal crowd supping bowls of coffee at Tinderbox. When you get to Tinderbox, make an undignified rush for the two airline seats – it's worth it! From Camden Passage, cross Upper Street and turn left. Tinderbox is a minute's walk down Upper Street, next to Lloyds Bank.

WHILE YOU'RE IN THE AREA

Criterion Islington   53 ESSEX ROAD, LONDON N1 2BN   ℂ 020 7359 5707
www.criterion-auctioneers.co.uk   ▶ 95
Continue through Camden Passage and along Essex Road. About 500 yards/450 metres ahead, on the left-hand side of the road between Dagmar Terrace and Cross Street, you will find Criterion Auctioneers. Criterion's price bracket is similar to that of Camden Passage, but you will find much more brown wood.

The Antique Trader   THE MILLINERY WORKS, 87 SOUTHGATE ROAD,
LONDON N1 3JS   ℂ 020 7359 2019   *www.millineryworks.co.uk*   ▶ 113
The Antique Trader is not far away but is best visited by taxi.

Sadler's Wells   ROSEBERY AVENUE, LONDON EC1R 4TN
ℂ 020 7863 8198   *www.sadlerswells.com*
In June 1683, Thomas Sadler built a 'musick' house to entertain visitors who took the waters (which were believed to be medicinal) from a medieval well in the grounds of his house. Today, Sadler's Wells is housed in a modern building and hosts some of the best dance and theatre in London. From Angel tube station, walk down St John Street (the continuation of Upper Street) away from Camden Passage, and then turn right at Rosebery Avenue.

2 Auction Houses

Everyone's heard of Bonhams, Christie's and Sotheby's. The formal nature of these great auction houses can be intimidating to newcomers, but the experience is definitely one not to be missed! Previews and auctions are free and open to the public. This is an excellent opportunity to examine pieces in a 'hands-on' manner and get a good feel for prices.

FIVE TIPS FOR BUYING AT AUCTION HOUSES

1. Always preview the auction with enough time to look properly at the pieces in which you are interested. If a piece is under something else or hard to see, ask a saleroom porter to get it out for you to inspect more closely. (There's nothing worse than realizing your new purchase has a broken leg or scratched top.)

2. You can always ask for a condition report from the auctioneer. A condition report is where the auctioneer should tell you about the general condition, mentioning any previous alterations and restorations.

3. Decide a budget for bidding and stick to it. You can always leave a commission bid (one which the auctioneer carries out on your behalf) if you think you may be tempted to bid higher on the day or will not be present at the auction.

4. Remember you will have to pay the buyer's premium, which is often about 20% of the final hammer price.

5. Check how much time you have to arrange collection after the auction. Many auction houses begin to charge you for storage within a day or two of the sale if the piece is not collected.

BONHAMS

Bonhams New Bond Street 101 NEW BOND STREET, LONDON W1S 1SR
℡ 020 7629 6602 *www.bonhams.com*
Bonhams was founded in 1793 by antique print dealer Thomas Dodd and book specialist Walter Bonham. In the 19th century, Bonhams expanded to include the fine and decorative art sales that it has today. Bonhams purchased Phillips Auctioneers in 2001 and now boasts a formidable number of sales, ranging from fine quality to more affordable decorative auctions. During the season, auctions can be viewed up to four days before the sale.

Bonhams Knightsbridge MONTPELIER STREET, LONDON SW7 1HH
℡ 020 7393 3900 *www.bonhams.com*
This venue of Bonhams auctions less expensive fine and decorative art. Although there will be items with estimates of a few thousand pounds, you can often purchase here for under £1,000. Auctions can be viewed up to two to three days before the sale.

CHRISTIE'S

Christie's King Street 8 KING STREET, LONDON SW1Y 6QT
℡ 020 7839 9060 *www.christies.com*
James Christie began auctioning in 1766, quickly becoming – together with Sotheby's – the premier auctioneer in England. Vast amounts of goods have come under the hammer here, much of which has been consigned by aristocracy and even royalty.

Today, Christie's still auctions some of the finest antiques and works of art in the world, and the King Street branch is its venue for the highest-quality pieces sold in Europe. There are sales year-round in a plethora of categories. The four days immediately prior to an auction tend to be viewing days

Christie's South Kensington 85 OLD BROMPTON ROAD, LONDON SW7 3LD
℡ 020 7930 6074 *www.christies.com*
This branch of Christie's auctions more collectible and less important art and antiques. Nonetheless, items can still sell for tens or even hundreds of thousands of pounds. There are more sales and more subjects sold at South Kensington than at King Street, and viewings usually take place over the two to three days prior to the sale.

CRITERION

Criterion Islington 53 ESSEX ROAD, LONDON N1 2BN
℡ 020 7359 5707 *www.criterion-auctioneers.co.uk*
Criterion's price bracket is similar to that of **Camden Passage**. However, you will find much more brown wood, including chests, tables, chairs and other traditional furniture. Viewing times are 2 p.m. until 7 p.m. on Fridays, 10 a.m. to 6 p.m. on Saturdays and Sundays, and 10 a.m. to 4 p.m. on Mondays, and the sale starts at 5 p.m.

Criterion Riverside Auctions 41–47 CHATFIELD ROAD, LONDON SW11
℡ 020 7228 5563 *www.criterionauctions.co.uk/riverside*
Capitalizing on its north London success, Criterion opened new auction rooms south of the river in 2004. With general antiques and modern furnishings offered on a weekly basis, it is one to watch. Sales are held on Mondays at 5 p.m., with viewings on Fridays (10 a.m.–7 p.m.), Saturdays and Sundays (10 a.m.–6 p.m.), and Mondays from 10 a.m.

LOTS ROAD

71–73 LOTS ROAD, LONDON SW10 0RN ℡ 020 7376 6800 *www.lotsroad.com*
Each Sunday, this Chelsea auction house has two sales of modern and antique furniture respectively. On the whole, the price bracket is less expensive than Christie's, Sotheby's and Bonhams. The quality tends to be more decorative than fine, but for those interested in buying reasonably priced antiques, this is a good call. Viewings start on Thursday morning and continue every day until the modern auction begins on Sunday at 2 p.m. Best buys are modern furniture sold by ex-pats leaving London.

ROSEBERY'S

74–76 KNIGHTS HILL, LONDON SE27 0JD ℡ 020 8761 2522 *www.roseberys.co.uk*
A relative newcomer to the London auction scene, Rosebery's was established in 1988 and moved to its West Norwood premises in 1998. Filling a gap in the market for auc-

tions of mid-range pieces, Rosebery's now holds thirty-six auctions a year, covering furniture, decorative arts, paintings, silver, ceramics, jewelry and textiles.

Take the overland train from Victoria station (Victoria, District and Circle lines) to West Norwood. Exit on to Knights Hill, cross the street, turn left and walk about 200 yards/180 metres until you see the large Rosebery's building on your right.

SOTHEBY'S

Sotheby's New Bond Street 34–35 NEW BOND STREET, LONDON W1A 2AA
℗ 020 7293 5000 *www.sothebys.com*
Older than its rival Christie's, Sotheby's was founded in 1744 as an antiquarian book auctioneer. Today, Sotheby's sells some of the most important and most expensive art and antiques in the world. The very best, in terms of quality and price, is sold at Bond Street. The four days before a sale tend to be viewing days. Sotheby's New Bond Street also houses a smart in-house café/restaurant where you can relax and soak up the elegant atmosphere.

Sotheby's Olympia OLYMPIA 2, HAMMERSMITH ROAD, LONDON W14 8UX
℗ 020 7293 5555 *www.sothebys.com*
Sotheby's second venue for the sale of slightly less valuable antiques has large show-rooms and a pleasant café. The tube to Olympia (Kensington on the District line) is often infrequent, causing some dealers to joke about viewing Sotheby's 'Oblivion', but your perseverance in getting there will be well worth the effort. Sales are on display for up to one week before the auction. A real joy of viewing Sotheby's Olympia is the free two hour parking in the Olympia car park. Be sure to park in a Sotheby's bay and ask the front desk to validate your ticket.

SPINK

69 SOUTHAMPTON ROW, LONDON WC1B 4ET ℗ 020 7563 4000 *www.spink.com*
Spink was founded in 1666 and started to deal in coins in 1703. It didn't hold its first coin auction until 1978. The company expanded in 1996 when Christie's stamp department was integrated into Spink. In 1999, Spink achieved the world record price for a British coin when a lot went for a staggering £170,500. Today, Spink is located in the old Post Office building in Bloomsbury. If you're into coins, banknotes, medals, stamps, books, medal services and special commissions, then this is the place for you! Spink is open between 9.30 a.m. and 5.30 p.m. Monday to Friday, and every item up for auction is usually on display for several days before a sale.

3 Antique Fairs

London's antique fairs cater for all budgets and interests. At one end of the market, you can find less expensive antiques which might only be sold by dealers who travel between fairs and markets. At the other end (for example, at Grosvenor House), elite dealers bring their finest pieces, many of which have been held back throughout the year for this one fair.

At fairs you can browse through the stock of dozens of dealers, seeing what is available and getting a feel for market prices without the formality or effort of visiting individual shops. Accordingly, many people time buying trips to coincide with one or more of the major fairs. Log on to the fairs' websites to determine specific dates and times.

FIVE TIPS FOR BUYING AT ANTIQUE FAIRS

1. If you are a dealer, always bring a business card and ask if there is free entry for trade.

2. Arrive early so that you may be the first to find that under-priced gem.

3. Especially at less formal fairs, bring cash to increase your bargaining power.

4. If you love something but cannot quite justify the price, leave it. If it is still available at the end of the fair, make an offer.

5. Almost all fairs will have a shippers' area. They will collect and deliver your purchases locally or abroad. This is often necessary for larger items.

ALEXANDRA PALACE

ALEXANDRA PALACE WAY, THE GREAT HALL, WOOD GREEN, LONDON N22 7AY
℗ 020 8883 7061 *www.pigandwhistlepromotions.com www.alexandrapalace.com*
Alexandra Palace (the building) is a quintessentially Victorian construction. One hundred and twenty-four thousand people visited the marvellous 'People's Palace' within sixteen days of its opening in 1873. It then promptly burnt down. Rebuilt and reopened within two years, Ally Pally (as it is affectionately known by local residents) sits within the 196-acre Alexandra Park. Sitting on a hill due north of central London, it enjoys fabulous views of the capital.

Ally Pally (the fair) takes place on Sundays in January, March, September and November each year. The dealers offer a vast array of antiques, with a particular strength in late 19th-century and early 20th-century British decorative arts. Prices range from a few pounds to several thousand.

To get there by public transport, take the Piccadilly line to Wood Green station. From there, either walk about a mile (1.6 km) to Ally Pally or take the W3 bus from bus stop 'F'. Alternatively, overland trains to Alexandra Palace station run from Moorgate station in the City of London business district or King's Cross (with a change at Finsbury Park).

ARDINGLY

SOUTH OF ENGLAND SHOWGROUND, ARDINGLY, WEST SUSSEX
℗ 01636 605 107 *www.dmgantiquefairs.com*
Ardingly is not strictly in London, but neither are three of London's airports! Expect to find a wide range of prices and quality of furniture, ceramics, textiles, architectural pieces and collectibles. Entry is £20 on Tuesdays and £5 on Wednesdays. Annoyingly, many dealers cut the first day short and do not return for the second, so your best bet is to get there early. The fair takes place six times a year (i.e. every other month) on Tuesdays and Wednesdays. To get there by public transport, take the train from London Victoria (Victoria, District and Circle lines) to Hayward's Heath. The journey takes an hour. At Hayward's Heath, there is a courtesy bus service on Wednesdays.

THE BRITISH ANTIQUE DEALERS' ASSOCIATION FAIR

DUKE OF YORK'S HEADQUARTERS, ON THE DUKE OF YORK SQUARE, KING'S ROAD, LONDON SW3 4SD ✆ 020 7589 6108 *www.bada.org*
This upmarket London fair has traditional antiques of the highest quality from members of the British Antique Dealers' Association, the UK's most prestigious trade organization. The fair takes place once a year in March and lasts for about one week.

CHELSEA BROCANTE

CHELSEA TOWN HALL, KING'S ROAD, LONDON SW3 5EE
✆ 020 7254 4054 *www.adams-antiques-fairs.co.uk*
At this small decorative antique fair, you will find pretty antiques for decorating and collecting on a modest budget. There are usually **French painted** pieces as well as textiles and smalls. Prices range from a few pounds to several thousand pounds. This fair takes place on a Saturday twice during the winter and once in spring and autumn.

THE DECORATIVE ANTIQUES & TEXTILES FAIR (BATTERSEA)

THE MARQUEE, BATTERSEA PARK ✆ 020 7624 5173 OR
020 7223 2808 (DURING THE FAIR) *www.decorativefair.com*
The internationally renowned Battersea Decorative Antiques & Textiles Fair has become increasingly popular and upmarket over the years. You will find a wide range of decorative antiques, particularly French 19th century. The fair takes place three times a year in January, April and October and lasts for just under a week.

GROSVENOR HOUSE

GROSVENOR HOUSE, PARK LANE, LONDON W1K 7TN
✆ 020 7399 8100 *www.grosvenor-antiquesfair.co.uk*
The most prestigious art and antique fair in London, Grosvenor House is an annual event in the London summer season. It has dealers of only the highest quality in their specialist fields. You will encounter Chippendale furniture, fabulous paintings and Ancient artworks, often of a standard to rival the best museums. Even if prices are out of your budget (a few thousand to a few million pounds), the approach here is friendly, and there is no better place to train your eye to recognize the very best-quality antiques. The fair takes place in the first or second week of June and lasts for about one week.

Horti Hall

ROYAL HORTICULTURAL HALL'S LINDLEY HALL, ELVERTON STREET,
LONDON SW1P 2PF *www.adams-antiques-fairs.co.uk/HortiHall.htm*
This monthly Sunday fair is the largest of its type in London with plenty to keep you
occupied for an hour or two. The range of quality and styles tends to be brocante and
decorative rather than fine antiques. Prices range from a few pounds to a couple of
thousand pounds.

Olympia

HAMMERSMITH ROAD, LONDON W14 8UX
℗ 020 7370 8234 *www.olympia-antiques.com*
The summer, winter and spring Olympia fairs are annual events which each last for
about one week. The summer fair usually overlaps with Grosvenor House for a few
days (don't attempt both in one day!). Each fair tends to have an emphasis. The
winter fair is traditional, the spring fair is decorative including 20th century, and the
summer fair has the most exhibitors and the widest range of offerings.

The Olympia fairs are very prestigious and vetted. A vast range of periods and
genres are on offer, with an equally wide range of prices. Pieces can be a few hundred
pounds for a small drawing or ceramic piece to hundreds of thousands for paintings
and the highest-quality antique furniture.

Penman Antique Fairs

CHELSEA TOWN HALL, KING'S ROAD, LONDON SW3 5EE (SEPTEMBER)
KENSINGTON TOWN HALL, HORNTON STREET, LONDON W8 (JANUARY)
℗ 01825 744 074 *www.penman-fairs.co.uk*
Each of these medium-sized and high-quality antique fairs takes place once a year
(Chelsea in September, west London in January) and lasts several days. You can
expect to find pieces from a hundred pounds to a few thousand pounds at these
pleasant and approachable events with many dealers from outside London.

Sunbury

KEMPTON PARK RACECOURSE, KEMPTON PARK, SUNBURY-ON-THAMES,
MIDDLESEX TW16 5AQ ℗ 01932 230 946 *www.kemptonantiques.com*
This antique fair takes place from 7 a.m. to 2 p.m. on the second and last Tuesday
of every month. Lying south of Heathrow airport on the Thames, Sunbury is a large
and generally inexpensive trade fair with a wide range of decorative antiques and
collectibles. Standards vary, but this is often a very good event. Admission and
parking are free – joy!

4 Antique Markets

London's antique markets are usually held once a week, and each has its own specific day and times. The huge selection of items on offer ranges from truly interesting and rare pieces to collectibles, worthless knick-knacks and even modern reproductions. London's principal markets are Bermondsey, which is south of the Thames, St James's, near Piccadilly, and the more famous Covent Garden. At all of them you can expect to find locals and tourists, as well as typical British characters. Be sure to examine pieces closely at markets and bring cash to increase your bargaining ability. Whichever market you decide to visit, it is always best to get there as early as possible – most start to set up stalls in the early hours, and by lunchtime the show can often be over.

BERMONDSEY

LONG LANE, BERMONDSEY STREET, LONDON SE1 3UW

'Furthermore, in 1994 we abolished the ancient defence of purchase in market overt, which was a thieves' charter. Modesty prevents me from mentioning who introduced that Bill!' So said Lord Renton during a 1997 House of Lords debate on the international art market tabled by Lord Hindlip, Chairman of **Christie's**.

Bermondsey dealers arrive before dawn and sell their goods fast and cheap as the sun rises. This may explain Bermondsey's previous, notorious association with the centuries old law of market overt. The latter allowed buyers at markets established by charter or statute (and at every retail shop in the City of London) to obtain good title to stolen goods, provided those goods were purchased between sunrise and sunset and in accordance with the custom of the market.

WHILE YOU'RE IN THE BERMONDSEY AREA

There are several antiques warehouses located on Tower Bridge Road, a short walk from Bermondsey Market (heading towards Tower Bridge from the market). They sell a range of shipping goods. In the past, this meant traditional brown, mostly Edwardian furniture. Times are changing, however, and the Tower Bridge Road set are now blending in more **rustic** and modern pieces with their traditional offerings.

Tower Bridge Antiques International 71 TANNER STREET, LONDON SE1 3PL *℗* 020 7403 3660
Just around the corner from **salvage** dealers LASSCO is this massive warehouse which is packed over three floors with antiques, traditional and more modern shipping furniture. You can literally get lost in aisles of furniture stacked to the ceiling.

The Galleries 157 TOWER BRIDGE ROAD, LONDON SE1 3LW *℗* 020 7407 5372
A large selection of traditional English antiques and shipping furniture is on offer at this Bermondsey style business. There was talk of a new lease and a possible move to the country in the near future when the author last visited.

Capital Antiques 168A TOWER BRIDGE ROAD, LONDON SE1 3LS *℗* 020 7378 7263
A female-run, competitive antiques business which is more like a shop than a south London warehouse, Joan Carter has an ever-changing selection of English furniture encompassing Victorian, Edwardian and **Arts & Crafts** styles. Everything is neatly presented and priced to sell.

Europa House Antiques 160–164 TOWER BRIDGE ROAD, LONDON SE1 3LS

The Antiques Exchange 170–172 TOWER BRIDGE ROAD, LONDON SE1 3LS *℗* 020 7378 8828 *www.antiquesexchange.com*
This local auction house has sales of antique and reproduction furniture and objects, which take place at 2 p.m. on the first Sunday of every month.

The roots of Bermondsey Market go back to 1855 and Prince Albert, husband of Queen Victoria. Originally, the market took place on Islington's High Street, but it was forced to relocate when the old site was redeveloped. For this reason, it is sometimes known as New Caledonian Market. While the market itself focuses on collectibles, there are several furniture stores operating in the vicinity, which sometimes have real finds. This is definitely the gritty, wholesale end of the business.

You will find the market open for business from around 4 a.m. each Friday, and only novices arrive after 7 a.m. Although some close as early as 9 a.m., most stallholders stay open till around 2 p.m. Before sunrise, a taxi is undoubtedly the safest option. Ask to be let off at the corner of Long Lane and Bermondsey Street. The nearest tube station is London Bridge on the Northern line. Exit on to Tooley Street and walk past the London Dungeon until you come to Bermondsey Street. Turn right on Bermondsey Street, walk through the tunnel and continue for about 8–10 minutes until you reach Long Lane. At this point you will be able to see the market.

Manze's Café 87 TOWER BRIDGE ROAD, BERMONDSEY, LONDON SE1 4TW Ⓒ 020 7407 2985
The menu is small: all Manze's sells is pie, mash (potato), eels and liquer (pea sauce). Caving to modernity, Manze's now sells a vegetarian pie alongside the traditional meat pie. Everything is cheap, the food is tasty and the interior is fabulous, original Victorian with green and white tiles and workers' benches for seating. This is not for the faint-hearted or fussy eaters!

COVENT GARDEN

JUBILEE HALL, COVENT GARDEN, LONDON WC2E 7PG
This medium-sized antique market is particularly valued for its antiquarian prints. You can search through boxes organized by subject for whatever you desire – maps and scenes from various locations, architecture and natural history. There are also many individual dealers selling jewelry, silver and other trinkets. Many of these dealers do several of the various day markets around London, such as Bermondsey and St James's. This market is only open on Mondays from 7 a.m. to 5 p.m.

Take the tube to Covent Garden station (Piccadilly line). One part of the market is in the main, covered section of Covent Garden, and the other, Jubilee Market, is opposite on the South Piazza.

GREENWICH

GREENWICH MARKET, GREENWICH, LONDON SE10 9HZ *www.greenwich-market.co.uk*
Greenwich Market is the perfect place to go for collectibles and bric-a-brac, including coins, banknotes, medals, second-hand books and **Art Deco** furniture. It holds an antique market on Greenwich High Road on Saturdays and Sundays from 9 a.m. until 5 p.m. To get there by public transport, take the overland train from Charing Cross or the Docklands Light Railway to Greenwich.

Greenwich itself, on the banks of the Thames, is well worth a visit. Steeped in history, the Cutty Sark ('the last of the great Tea Clippers'), the National Maritime

Museum, the Old Royal Naval College on the banks of the Thames, the Royal Observatory (the original home of Greenwich Mean Time) and Greenwich Park (this is where the London Marathon starts each year) are all easily accessible. Make a day of it.

PORTOBELLO

PORTOBELLO ROAD, LONDON W11 ▶ 65–73

SPITALFIELDS

COMMERCIAL STREET, LONDON E1 6BG

The name of this market derives from the 12th-century St Mary Spital (a spital being a place where the sick were taken, a hospital). Most of the buildings in the area date from after the Great Fire in 1666, and the fine houses from the late 17th and early 18th centuries on nearby Fournier, Princelet and Wilkes Street were built by refugee French Huguenot silk weavers. (Huguenot refugees were often craftsmen who brought their skills in silversmithing and cabinetry from the French Court.)

Although the area and market of Spitalfields have ancient origins – the market was a fruit and vegetable market laid out in the 1680s and the current building dates from 1873 – this particular antique market is a relative newcomer, opened in May 2004. Building on the increasing interest and regeneration of the East End, the market offers general antiques, objects, ceramics, vintage clothing and militaria. It is the perfect stop for those working in the City and tourists alike and can easily be combined with lunch as there are several market stalls selling a range of food, including Asian, French and even Arkansas barbecue. The market is open from 8 a.m. to 3 p.m. every Thursday.

ST JAMES'S

COURTYARD, ST JAMES'S CHURCH, 197 PICCADILLY, LONDON W1J 9LL

This small but charming market mainly caters for tourists. There are about twenty to thirty stallholders with a range of small and inexpensive antiques, including prints, maps, jewelry, silver trinkets and other collectibles. You can easily go round the market in thirty minutes, and you may even be able to walk away with your own find for less than £20. This market is only open on Tuesdays from 8 a.m. to 6 p.m.

St James's Market takes place in the churchyard of St James's Piccadilly, a beautiful 17th-century Sir Christopher Wren church. Take the tube to Piccadilly Circus (Piccadilly and Bakerloo lines) and head for the Piccadilly exit. The church sits on Piccadilly and Jermyn Street, roughly 200 yards/180 metres from Piccadilly Circus. The following buses will also get you there: 6, 9, 12, 14, 15, 19 and 22.

World-renowned auction house **Christie's** (▶ 94), on King Street, is just around the corner from St James's Market and well worth a visit. Entry is free.

5 Style-by-Style

This section of the guide features recommended dealers for those collectors who are interested in a particular style or specialization. From pure English Georgian to Mid-Century Modern, this Style-by-Style guide shows you where to go to create a perfect, period interior. The various styles are listed alphabetically, although the dealers are grouped together by area following the Street-by-Street format.

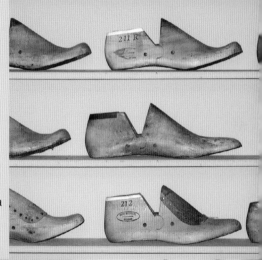

ART DECO

The term 'Art Deco' was coined at L'Exposition Internationale des Arts Décoratifs et Industriels Modernes in Paris in 1925. It refers to a forward-reaching artistic movement of the inter-war period, which utilized shapes and forms from industrialization and mechanization. Characteristics of Art Deco include streamlining, geometric patterns and bright colours, and it embodied a sense of optimism, luxury and glamour. Opulence is conveyed through expensive materials such as walnut, ivory and shagreen.

Art Deco is becoming more and more popular and collectible. The clean lines and modern feel complement modern interiors, and high-quality Art Deco pieces blend particularly well with other fine, period antiques.

WHERE TO GO

CHELSEA & FULHAM

Hemisphere 173 FULHAM ROAD, LONDON SW3 6JW ✆ 020 7581 9800 ▶ 20

Gordon Watson 50 FULHAM ROAD, LONDON SW3 6HH ✆ 020 7589 3108 ▶ 20

Fiona McDonald 97 MUNSTER ROAD, LONDON SW6 5RG
✆ 020 7731 3234 *www.fionamcdonald.com*
With Art Deco and modernist furniture, lighting and mirrors from the 1920s, 30s and 40s, Fiona McDonald is a purveyor extraordinaire of clean sophistication. Expect quality pieces displayed with panache.

Rupert Cavendish Antiques 610 KING'S ROAD, LONDON SW6 2DX
✆ 020 7731 7041 *www.rupertcavendish.co.uk* ▶ 30

BELGRAVIA

Ciancimino 99 PIMLICO ROAD, LONDON SW1W 8PH
✆ 020 7730 9950 *www.ciancimino.com* ▶ 35

Alexander von Moltke 46 BOURNE STREET, LONDON SW1W 8JD
✆ 020 7730 9020 *www.alexandervonmoltke.com* ▶ 38

Bob Lawrence Gallery 93 LOWER SLOANE STREET, LONDON SW1W 8DA
✆ 020 7730 5900 ▶ 39

KENSINGTON

Artemis Decorative Arts 36 KENSINGTON CHURCH STREET,
LONDON W8 4BX ✆ 020 7376 0377 ▶ 54

Kensington Church Street Antiques Centre, FCR Gallery 58–60 KENSINGTON
CHURCH STREET, LONDON W8 4DB *www.fcrgallery.com* ▶ 55

Pruskin Gallery 50 & 73 KENSINGTON CHURCH STREET,
LONDON W8 4BG ✆ 020 7937 1994 ► 55

NOTTING HILL

B & T Antiques 47 LEDBURY ROAD, LONDON W11 2AG
✆ 020 7229 7001 *www.bntantiques.co.uk* ► 72

MARYLEBONE

Alfie's Antique Market 13–25 CHURCH STREET, LONDON NW8 8DT
✆ 020 7723 6066 *www.alfiesantiques.com* ► 78

Marchand 14 CHURCH STREET, LONDON NW8 8EP ✆ 020 7724 9238 ► 79

Gallery 1930 18 CHURCH STREET, LONDON NW8 8EP ✆ 020 7723 1555
www.susiecooperceramics.com ► 79

Bizarre 24 CHURCH STREET, LONDON NW8 8EP ✆ 020 7724 1305
www.antiques-uk.co.uk/bizarre ► 79

Jazzy Art Deco 34 CHURCH STREET, LONDON NW8 8EP ✆ 020 7724 0837
www.jazzyartdeco.com ► 79

ISLINGTON

Mike Weedon 7 CAMDEN PASSAGE, LONDON N1 8EA ✆ 020 7226 5319
www.mikeweedonantiques.com ► 87

Style Gallery 10 CAMDEN PASSAGE, LONDON N1 8ED ✆ 020 7359 7867
www.styleantiques.co.uk ► 89

HOLBORN

Rennie's at French's Dairy 13 RUGBY STREET OFF LAMB'S CONDUIT,
LONDON WC1N 3QT ✆ 020 7405 0220 *www.rennart.co.uk*
Although not strictly an Art Deco specialist, Rennie's must be included in this
section for its enthusiasm and expertise in the British decorative and graphic arts
contemporary to the Art Deco movement in France. This quirky shop has a clear
interest in not only the visual elements of 1920s, 30s and 40s British design, but also
the social impetus. Expect posters, textiles, ceramics and some furniture. Quoting
Rennie's, 'It's special stuff for home and not too expensive'.

BATTERSEA

Banana Dance SHOP 20, THE NORTHCOTE ROAD ANTIQUES MARKET,
155A NORTHCOTE ROAD, LONDON SW11 6QT
✆ 01634 364 539 *www.bananadance.com*
The specialist dealers sell Art Deco ceramics, including Clarice Cliff and Suzy Cooper.

ART NOUVEAU

The Art Nouveau style developed in the 1880s and reached its height at the turn of the century. It is elaborate, expressive and a quintessential *fin de siècle* style. Art Nouveau is inspired by nature with curving, whiplash lines, and floral and female motifs. It is typified by stylized decoration with tendrils and sprout-like lines.

The French schools of Art Nouveau were more anachronistic, naturalistic and had some shared features with Rococo revival. In both France and Germany, the theme of the femme fatale arose with swirling hair, fairly-like features and elaborate robes (a stylized version of which is used for the Starbucks's logo).

The Glasgow School, however, was more geometric, drawing inspiration from Celtic designs. Its influence stretched to Vienna and Munich where Charles Rennie Mackintosh, pre-eminent Scottish Art Nouveau designer and graduate of the Glasgow School of Art, was often featured in the style magazine *The Studio*.

While the Glasgow School moved towards Puritanical style, simplicity and modernism, the French style became so staid as to be disdained and derided after 1910.

Many dealers listed under **Arts & Crafts** and **Art Deco** also sell Art Nouveau. Arts & Crafts dealers tend to have British furniture and objects with an Art Nouveau inspiration, whereas the Art Deco dealers often have continental pieces.

WHERE TO GO

MAYFAIR

Victor Arwas Gallery 3 CLIFFORD STREET, LONDON W1S 2LF
℗ 020 7734 3944 *www.victorarwas.com* ▶ 49

Liberty 210–220 REGENT STREET, LONDON W1B 5AH
℗ 020 7734 1234 *www.liberty.co.uk* ▶ 52
Opened by Sir Arthur Lasenby in 1875 with the aim of supplying useful and beautiful objects at prices within the reach of all classes, Liberty has a tendency to forget that last aim from time to time. Liberty has been closely associated with **Arts & Crafts** and Art Nouveau since the beginning and continues to carry textiles, wallpapers, antiques and reproductions in these styles. Liberty responded to the fashion for Art Nouveau by melding it with the tradition of British Arts & Crafts, resulting in Archibald Knox's Celtic revival Cymric-wares, Tudric-wares and Voysey's furniture and textiles. For an excellent selection of antique furniture, much of which was originally made for Liberty, visit the antiques department in the basement.

KENSINGTON

Kensington Church Street Antiques Centre 58–60 KENSINGTON CHURCH STREET, LONDON W8 4DB ℗ 020 7376 0425 ▶ 55
There are several specialists in Art Nouveau in this upmarket centre. JAG Decorative Arts (*www.jagdecorativearts.com*) sells Art Nouveau from the various European schools, including the Jugendstil, Secession, Darmstadt and Wiener Werkstätte. There is met-

alware, art glass, lighting and small furniture, making this an excellent call for the Art Nouveau collector and enthusiast. At FCR Gallery (*www.fcrgallery.com*), you will find 20th-century metalware, glass and ceramics including Art Nouveau.

Puritan Values 69 KENSINGTON CHURCH STREET, LONDON W8 4BG
℃ 020 7937 2410 *www.puritanvalues.co.uk* ▶ 55
You are most likely to find the particularly British interpretation of Art Nouveau at this decorative arts specialist.

NOTTING HILL

Jones Antique Lighting 194 WESTBOURNE GROVE, LONDON W11 2RH
℃ 020 7229 6866 ▶ 71
A good selection of early 20th-century Art Nouveau and **Art Deco** lighting is offered at this packed lighting shop.

ISLINGTON

Mike Weedon 7 CAMDEN PASSAGE, LONDON N1 8EA ℃ 020 7226 5319
www.mikeweedonantiques.com ▶ 87

Style Gallery 10 CAMDEN PASSAGE, LONDON N1 8ED ℃ 020 7359 7867
www.styleantiques.co.uk ▶ 89

MUSWELL HILL

Crafts Nouveau 112 ALEXANDRA PARK ROAD, LONDON N10 2AE
℃ 020 8444 3300 *www.craftsnouveau.co.uk*
In the **Arts & Crafts** north London neighbourhood of Muswell Hill, this antique shop displays its absolute passion for both Arts & Crafts and Art Nouveau. There is a large selection of furniture and objects in both styles and at very reasonable prices. Use the journey planner at *www.tfl.gov.uk* or take what will be a fairly long taxi ride.

ARTS & CRAFTS

The Arts & Crafts movement was a particularly British movement which began as a reaction to the increasing mechanization and mass production of industrial design in the mid-19th century. In contrast to that, the founders of the Arts & Crafts movement looked back to medieval craftsmanship. Designers such as William Morris were also inspired by the Great Exhibition of 1851 and began to knit their design ideas closely with their political interests in romanticized socialism. Their ultimate goal was good design, high quality and non-mechanized craftsmanship which used native materials to make furniture and other objects for the common man. Unfortunately, the basic premise of making high-quality, hand-crafted pieces for the average man was not possible and, in the end, it was only the wealthy who could afford 'humble' Arts & Crafts.

Although the earliest Arts & Crafts pieces were made in the 1850s, the style only became popular and widespread from around 1890 onwards. From about that time many pieces were made by machine, sometimes using mechanization to create the look of being hand-crafted. The popularity of Arts & Crafts waned around the time of World War I. Its basic principles of honest design, craftsmanship and the use of native materials were kept alive, however, by the Cotswold School and by Robert 'Mouseman' Thompson, whose family continues to operate his workshop (*www.robertthompsons.co.uk*).

Until rather recently, Arts & Crafts furniture in England was not particularly admired or respected for a variety of reasons. From not being old enough or smart enough to simply not being 18th century (the period which is regarded as the pinnacle of English furniture), Arts & Crafts was not a style that a 'good' dealer would sell. Things have changed, and there is now a widespread acceptance of the importance and quality of the style.

London is now home to several specialist dealers who cater to the growing interest in the Arts & Crafts movement. There are two general areas where you will find Arts & Crafts specialist dealers: first in central London's **Mayfair** and **Kensington**, and second in north London due to local demand created within nearby neighbourhoods built in the Arts & Crafts style.

WHERE TO GO

MAYFAIR

H. Blairman & Sons 119 MOUNT STREET, LONDON W1K 3NL
℃ 020 7493 0444 *www.blairman.co.uk* ▶ 50

Liberty 210–220 REGENT STREET, LONDON W1B 5AH ℃ 020 7734 1234
www.liberty.co.uk ▶ 52

KENSINGTON

Paul Reeves 32B KENSINGTON CHURCH STREET, LONDON W8 4HA
℃ 020 7937 1594 *www.paulreeveslondon.com* ▶ 54

Puritan Values 69 KENSINGTON CHURCH STREET, LONDON W8 4BG
© 020 7937 2410 *www.puritanvalues.co.uk* ▶ 55

Haslam and Whiteway 105 KENSINGTON CHURCH STREET,
LONDON W8 7LN © 020 7229 1145 ▶ 58

ISLINGTON

The Antique Trader THE MILLINERY WORKS, 87 SOUTHGATE ROAD,
LONDON N1 3JS © 020 7359 2019 *www.millineryworks.co.uk*
This fabulous Arts & Crafts specialist is relatively easy to get to from Camden Town's
Art Furniture (see below) and is worth the effort. The Antique Trader is an absolute
must for any Arts & Crafts enthusiast because of the owners' extensive knowledge,
stock and regular exhibitions. The back catalogues from these exhibitions include
subjects such as Ambrose Heal, the Glasgow Style, the Cotswold House and the
Liberty Style and constitute excellent reference material. At The Antique Trader you
will find a large stock of Arts & Crafts, and Aesthetic and Gothic revival furniture and
objects, and very knowledgeable and friendly dealers. The Antique Trader is not too far
from Islington's **Camden Passage**, but is best visited by taxi.

CAMDEN

Art Furniture 158 CAMDEN STREET, LONDON NW1 9PA
© 020 7267 4324 *www.artfurniture.co.uk*
Art Furniture is located under railway arches in Camden Town and comprises three
dealers specializing in all things Arts & Crafts. This was one of London's first shops to
specialize in the Arts & Crafts style, and the dealers have fifteen years' experience and
knowledge. This is clear from their large range of reasonably priced furniture, lighting,
art, ceramics and objects. The dealers at Art Furniture are very helpful and customer-
friendly. Almost all of their pieces are quickly listed on the website with photos,
descriptions, measurements and prices. Art Furniture is open seven days a week from
12 p.m. until 5 p.m.
   By tube, exit Camden Town (Northern line) station on to Camden Road and walk
past Sainsbury's supermarket. At the first set of traffic lights, at Camden Street, turn
left. Ahead of you, on the right-hand side of the road just under the railway line, you
will see the door for Art Furniture.

MUSWELL HILL

Crafts Nouveau 112 ALEXANDRA PARK ROAD, LONDON N10 2AE
© 020 8444 3300 *www.craftsnouveau.co.uk* ▶ 111

ALSO OF INTEREST

The De Morgan Centre 38 WEST HILL, LONDON SW18 1RZ
© 020 8871 1144 *www.demorgan.org.uk*
Enter through Wandsworth Library to see the impressive collection of ceramics by
William De Morgan and paintings by his wife, Evelyn De Morgan. The De Morgan

Centre is the perfect stop for the Arts & Crafts enthusiast. It is open Monday to Wednesday from 12 p.m. to 6 p.m. and Friday and Saturday from 10 a.m. to 5 p.m. The nearest stations are Wandsworth Town (accessible by rail from Waterloo station) and Putney (East Putney on the District line).

William Morris Gallery LLOYD PARK, FOREST ROAD, LONDON E17 4PP
℗ 020 8527 3782 *www.lbwf.gov.uk/wmg*
This museum is located in what was the Morris family's home, an 18th-century manor house in Walthamstow (in those days this was 'the country'). The collection shows the life, work and influence of William Morris and boasts an impressive collection of furniture, fabrics, wallpapers and stained glass designed by Morris and his followers.

To arrive by public transport, take the Victoria line to Walthamstow Central. Upon exiting, take any bus from stop 'C' to Bell Corner and then walk a few moments west on Forest Row. The Gallery is a large period house on your right.

Asian Style

Ever since Queen Mary collected Chinese blue and white porcelain in the late 17th century, using it to decorate her palaces at Kensington and Hampton Court, the British have had a wonderful affection for Asian decorative arts.

In the 18th century, Britain undertook an enormous volume of trade with China, particularly with the kilns of Jingdezhen and the port city of Canton. It is estimated that in the 18th century England alone imported one to two million pieces of Chinese porcelain a year. No country house was complete without a display of Chinese blue and white porcelain. Since then, large amounts of decorative arts have been taken out of China, not least due to the turmoil created by the Boxer Rebellion (1900), war with Japan (1894–95 and 1937–45), the Civil War (1945–49) and the Cultural Revolution (1966–76). Much of this found its way to Britain. As the British have collected Asian decorative arts and antiques for over three hundred years, it should be no surprise that London is a major world centre for Asian arts and antiques.

In the late 19th and early 20th centuries, George Salting and Sir Percival David amassed collections of the finest-quality Chinese ceramics, organizing exhibitions and displays in London. These collections are now housed at the Victoria & Albert Museum (▶ 24) and the Percival David Foundation of Chinese Art located in a charming 18th-century Bloomsbury town house (*www.pdfmuseum.org.uk*) respectively. Together with the collection at the British Museum (*www.thebritishmuseum.ac.uk*), today they are second only to the Imperial Collection housed in the National Palace Museum Taipei and contain some of the rarest and most important pieces in this field.

The collective knowledge and connoisseurship of London's Asian antique dealers is enormous. It results from London's long history of dealing in quality Asian decorative arts and antiques (many dealers in this field are second or even third generation), as well as from the availability of London's wonderful academic reference collections. Together with the sheer number of dealers, the variety and in many cases rarity of items on offer, London is a wonderful centre to visit for connoisseurs of Asian decorative arts and antiques.

If you are around in London during the second week of November, be sure to attend some of the many interesting events organized during the 'Asian Art in London' week (*www.asianartinlondon.com*). From dealers to museums and auctions houses, there are dozens of lectures, events and open evenings which highlight London's authority and resources in Asian arts. Asian antique dealers tend to be based in **St James's**, **Mayfair** and **Kensington Church Street**.

WHERE TO GO

ST JAMES'S

Brian Harkins 3 BURY STREET, LONDON SW1Y 6AB
℃ 020 7839 3338 ▶ 43

Jonathan Tucker Antonia Tozer Asian Art 37 BURY STREET,
LONDON SW1Y 6AU ℃ 020 7839 3414 *www.asianartresource.co.uk* ▶ 44

Malcolm Fairley 40 BURY STREET, LONDON SW1Y 6AU
© 020 7930 8770 ▶ 44

Kenneth Davis 15 KING STREET, LONDON SW1Y 6QU
© 020 7930 0313 ▶ 44

Priestley & Ferraro 17 KING STREET, LONDON SW1Y 6QU
© 020 7930 6228 *www.priestleyandferraro.com* ▶ 44

Simon Ray Indian & Islamic Works of Art 21 KING STREET,
LONDON SW1Y 6QY © 020 7930 5500 *www.simonray.com* ▶ 44

Asian Art Gallery – Christopher Bruckner 8 DUKE STREET,
LONDON SW1Y 6BN © 020 7930 0204 ▶ 44

MAYFAIR

Eskenazi 10 CLIFFORD STREET, LONDON W1S 2LH © 020 7493 5464
www.eskenazi.co.uk ▶ 49

Robert Hall 15C CLIFFORD STREET, LONDON W1S 4JZ © 020 7734 4008
www.snuffbottle.com ▶ 49

Gordon Reece Gallery 16 CLIFFORD STREET, LONDON W1S 3RG
© 020 7439 0007 *www.gordonreecegalleries.com* ▶ 49

A & J Speelman Oriental Art 129 MOUNT STREET, LONDON W1K 3NX
© 020 7499 5126 *www.ajspeelman.com* ▶ 50

Gerard Hawthorn 104 MOUNT STREET, LONDON W1K 2TJ
© 020 7409 2888 ▶ 50

Grace Wu Bruce 12A BALFOUR MEWS, LONDON W1K 2BJ
© 020 7499 3750 ▶ 51

Sydney L. Moss 51 BROOK STREET, LONDON W1K 4HP
© 020 7629 4670 *www.slmoss.com* ▶ 51

Jan Van Beers Oriental Art 34 DAVIES STREET, LONDON W1K 4NE
© 020 7408 0434 *www.janvanbeers.com* ▶ 52

KENSINGTON

R. and G. McPherson Antiques 40 KENSINGTON CHURCH STREET,
LONDON W8 4BX © 020 7937 0812 *www.orientalceramics.com* ▶ 60

Japanese Gallery 66D KENSINGTON CHURCH STREET, LONDON W8 4BY
© 020 7229 2934 *www.japanesegallery.co.uk* ▶ 60

Cohen & Cohen 101B KENSINGTON CHURCH STREET, LONDON W8 7LN
© 020 7727 7677 *www.cohenandcohen.co.uk* ▶ 60

Jorge Welsh Oriental Porcelain & Works of Art 116 KENSINGTON CHURCH STREET, LONDON W8 4BH ℂ 020 7229 2140 *www.jorgewelsh.com* ► 60

Millner Manolatos 2 CAMPDEN STREET, LONDON W8 7EP ℂ 020 7229 3268 *www.arthurmillner.com* ► 60

S. Marchant 120 KENSINGTON CHURCH STREET, LONDON W8 4BH ℂ 020 7229 5319 *www.marchantasianart.com* ► 60

Geoffrey Waters 133 KENSINGTON CHURCH STREET, LONDON W8 7PL ℂ 020 7243 6081 *www.antique-chinese-porcelain.com* ► 62

J. A. N. Fine Art 134 KENSINGTON CHURCH STREET, LONDON W8 4BH ℂ 020 7792 0736 *www.jan-fineart-london.com* ► 62

Gregg Baker Asian Art 132 KENSINGTON CHURCH STREET, LONDON W8 4BN ℂ 020 7221 3533 *www.japanesescreens.com* ► 62

Peter Kemp 170 KENSINGTON CHURCH STREET, LONDON W8 4BN ℂ 020 7229 2988 ► 62

ISLINGTON

Kevin Page Oriental Art 2–6 CAMDEN PASSAGE, LONDON N1 8ED ℂ 020 7226 8558 *www.kevinpage.co.uk* ► 87

GEORGIAN STYLE

English cabinet-making was at its height during the 18th and early 19th centuries. Famous designers included Chippendale, Sheraton, Hepplewhite and Gillow. This apogee of cabinetry can be attributed to several factors. One driving force was the mass immigration of almost 50,000 Huguenots from the French court of Louis XIV to England. They were fleeing oppression after the revocation of the Edict of Nantes in 1685, which had granted rights to Protestants. Many Huguenots were highly skilled craftsmen, and their arrival heralded a new era in English decorative arts. Of particular fame was Daniel Marot, architect and designer to the king in Holland and England.

The second factor was England's trade with the New World in the 18th century. This trade in items such as wood, tobacco, tea, spices and slaves fuelled a new, wealthy merchant class which required furniture and objects to fill their new homes. Also, mahogany imported from the New World had different characteristics to native woods; it lent itself to sharply carved decoration and highly figured veneers, both of which became hallmarks of English mid-18th-century furniture.

One final factor was the comprehensive book of furniture designs published by Thomas Chippendale in 1754, 1755 and 1762 as *The Gentleman and Cabinet-Maker's Director*. This book was circulated extensively and influenced furniture makers all over England, Ireland and Scotland.

Eighteenth- and early 19th-century English furniture is possibly the most coveted and expensive genre of antiques. When prices frequently break the £10,000 mark and even run into hundreds of thousands of pounds, expert knowledge is crucial, and the English antiques trade is arguably the most knowledgeable in the world. Many London dealers are second or third generation with a vast amount of family knowledge, training and history from which to draw.

Also, many English dealers do a considerable amount of their business at major fairs, where their pieces are vetted by committees of fellow experts. At fairs such as Grosvenor House and Olympia (▶ 99–100), vetting committees are tough. Committee members simply will not allow a fellow dealer to show a piece that is not what it purports to be.

The dealers who specialize in fine English furniture and works of art tend to be located together in three of London's most important and well-known areas for antiques: **Fulham Road**, **Mayfair** and **Kensington Church Street**. If you are on a restricted budget, this is a difficult area in which to collect, but prices tend to be less expensive on Fulham Road and Kensington Church Street than in prestigious Mayfair.

WHERE TO GO

CHELSEA & SOUTH KENSINGTON

Robert Miller Fine Art 15 GLENDOWER PLACE, LONDON SW7 3DR
℗ 020 7584 4733 ▶ 20

Anthony James & Son 88 FULHAM ROAD, LONDON SW3 6HR
℗ 020 7584 1120 *www.anthony-james.com* ▶ 20

Michael Hughes UPSTAIRS AT 88 FULHAM ROAD, LONDON SW3 6HR
✆ 020 7589 0660 ▸ 20

Godson & Coles 92 FULHAM ROAD, LONDON SW3 6HR ✆ 020 7584 2200 ▸ 20

Michael Foster 118 FULHAM ROAD, LONDON SW3 6HU ✆ 020 7373 3636 ▸ 21

Robert Dickson and Lesley Rendall 263 FULHAM ROAD, LONDON SW3 6HY
✆ 020 7351 0330 *www.dicksonrendall-antiques.co.uk* ▸ 21

Apter Fredericks 265–267 FULHAM ROAD, LONDON SW3 6HY
✆ 020 7352 2188 *www.apter-fredericks.com* ▸ 21

Peter Lipitch 120 FULHAM ROAD, LONDON SW3 6HU ✆ 020 7373 3328 ▸ 21

ST JAMES'S

Harris Lindsay 67 JERMYN STREET, LONDON SW1Y 6NY ✆ 020 7839 5767 ▸ 43

John Bly 27 BURY STREET, LONDON SW1Y 6AL
✆ 07831 888 825 *www.johnbly.com* ▸ 43

MAYFAIR

Partridge Fine Art 144–146 NEW BOND STREET, LONDON W1S 2PF
✆ 020 7629 0834 *www.partridgefinearts.com* ▸ 47

Mallett 141 NEW BOND STREET, LONDON W1S 2BS
✆ 020 7499 7411 *www.mallett.co.uk* ▸ 47

Ronald Phillips 26 BRUTON STREET, LONDON W1J 6LQ ✆ 020 7493 2341 ▸ 49

M. Turpin 27 BRUTON STREET, LONDON W1X 6QN
✆ 020 7493 3275 *www.mturpin.co.uk* ▸ 49

Alistair Sampson Antiques 120 MOUNT STREET, LONDON W1K 3NN
✆ 020 7409 1799 *www.alistairsampson.com* ▸ 50

H. Blairman & Sons 119 MOUNT STREET, LONDON W1K 3NL
✆ 020 7493 0444 *www.blairman.co.uk* ▸ 50

Mount Street Galleries 93 MOUNT STREET, LONDON W1K 1SY
✆ 020 7493 1613 ▸ 50

Pelham Galleries 24 & 25 MOUNT STREET, LONDON W1K 2RR
✆ 020 7629 0905 ▸ 51

Michael Lipitch ✆ 0773 095 4347
For the rarest and finest-quality pieces of English 18th-century furniture and works of art befitting connoisseurs and museums, serious buyers can reach this third-generation dealer on the number above.

SMITH'S
TERRESTRIAL GLOBE
Containing the whole of
THE LATEST DISCOVERIES
AND
Geographical Improvements
also the TRACKS of
the most celebrated Circumnavigators
LONDON

KENSINGTON

Neil Wibroe & Natasha MacIlwaine 77 KENSINGTON CHURCH STREET, LONDON W8 4BG ℰ 020 7937 2461 ▶ 55

Reindeer Antiques 81 KENSINGTON CHURCH STREET, LONDON W8 4BG ℰ 020 7937 3754 *www.reindeerantiques.co.uk* ▶ 58

Brian Rolleston Antiques 104A KENSINGTON CHURCH STREET, LONDON W8 4BU ℰ 020 7229 5892 ▶ 58

Eddy Bardawil 106 KENSINGTON CHURCH STREET, LONDON W8 4BH ℰ 020 7221 3967 ▶ 58

Patrick Sandberg Antiques 150–152 KENSINGTON CHURCH STREET, LONDON W8 4BN ℰ 020 7229 0373 *www.antiquefurniture.net* ▶ 59

Butchoff Antiques 154 KENSINGTON CHURCH STREET, LONDON W8 4BN ℰ 020 7221 8174 *www.butchoff.com* ▶ 59

Butterworth Ltd ℰ 07850 958 210 *www.butterworthltd.com*
If you are a designer or collector and in the area, be sure to call Adrian Butterworth, a likeable and knowledgeable dealer, to view his fine collection.

KNIGHTSBRIDGE

Hotspur 14 LOWNDES STREET, LONDON SW1X 9EX ℰ 020 7235 1918
Hotspur offers gilt and cut glass, bold Georgian furniture and gorgeous art objects.

Jeremy 29 LOWNDES STREET, LONDON SW1X 9HX ℰ 020 7823 2923 *www.jeremy.ltd.uk*
Jeremy sells the very finest furniture, chandeliers and works of art.

Norman Adams 8–10 HANS ROAD, LONDON SW3 1RX *www.normanadams.com*
Literally a few steps from Harrods, Norman Adams boasts fine English antiques with a country-house feel – or old-fashioned ambience and a relaxed approach in its lofty showrooms, to use its own words. In either case, you can rest assured of a friendly welcome and gorgeous offerings.

Mid-Century Modern
and Contemporary

The 20th century brought new styles, materials and techniques to furniture making which either lent themselves to, or were made possible by, new mechanical processes. Plywood, tubular steel, plastic, perspex, chrome, aluminium, fibreglass and glass all entered the furniture maker's workshop. Throughout the mid-20th century, however, a delicious irony arose. While these new materials permitted an abundance of new forms, furniture would for decades embody the philosophy of modernism, and function – not form – would be paramount.

In previous centuries, furniture making's driving force had been craftsmen displaying their skill through the creation of beautiful, often intricate, forms. In the 20th century, however, craftsmen were displaced by mechanization and quickly usurped by furniture designers. The latter sought to display their new philosophy through the creation of functional, often simple, designs.

A rule of thumb has always been that a piece must be over one hundred years old to be 'antique'. For better or worse this rule is breaking down in common usage. New dealers and collectors are increasingly beginning to select furniture and objects from the 1920s to the 1970s based on good and/or interesting design. While big names such as Herman Miller, Eames and Saarinen are instantly recognizable and command serious prices, there are still bargains to be had.

WHERE TO GO

CHELSEA

David Gill   60 FULHAM ROAD, LONDON SW3 6HH   ℂ 020 7589 5946   ▶ 20

Babylon   301 FULHAM ROAD, LONDON SW10 9QH   ℂ 020 7376 7233   ▶ 22

Core One   THE GASWORKS, GATE D, 2 MICHAEL ROAD, LONDON SW6 2AN
ℂ 020 7371 5700   ▶ 31

NOTTING HILL

Berg Brothers   109 FRESTON ROAD, LONDON W11 4BD   ℂ 020 7313 6590
Slightly off the beaten track in trendy **Notting Hill**, this unusual shop stocks mid-century modern, 1960s and 70s furniture, lighting and objects. Bright colours and surprisingly good design from the past fifty years will leave you pondering a complete style makeover for your own home.

Themes & Variations   231 WESTBOURNE GROVE, LONDON W11 2SE
ℂ 020 7727 5531   *www.themesandvariations.com*
The perfect shop for those with the mid-century modern bug and/or an interest in contemporary designers, Themes & Variations is part furniture shop, part art gallery, with everything exuding bright and bold modernity.

Plywood2Plastic ✆ 07768 025 320 *www.ply2plastic.co.uk*
In a **Notting Hill** warehouse-style set-up, 20th-century dealer Nigel Wells offers mid-century modern furniture and lighting which is mainly American, with makers such as Eames and Nelson, as well as high-end European. Call for an appointment.

MARYLEBONE

Nick Haywood 9 CHURCH STREET, LONDON NW8 8EE ✆ 020 7224 9629 ▶ 78

Alfie's Antique Market 13–25 CHURCH STREET, LONDON NW8 8DT
✆ 020 7723 6066 *www.alfiesantiques.com* ▶ 78

ISLINGTON

Origin 25 CAMDEN PASSAGE, LONDON N1 8EA ✆ 020 7704 1326
www.origin101.co.uk ▶ 89

Fandango Interiors 50 CROSS STREET, LONDON N1 2BA
✆ 020 7226 1777 *www.fandango.uk.com*
Fandango stocks ultra-sleek Danish modern and chrome furniture from the 60s and 70s complemented by carefully selected objects, lighting and artworks for the all-out modernist interior.

Back in Time 93 HOLLOWAY ROAD, LONDON N7 8LT
✆ 020 7700 0744 *www.backintimeuk.com*
Local Highbury and Islington specialist dealer Back in Time is a great resource for reasonably priced, funky furniture and fun style from the 50s to the 70s.

CAMDEN TOWN

At the Chalk Farm end of Camden Market (better known for outrageous clothes and Bohemian crafts), you will find Stables Market with specialist dealers in vintage and cutting-edge collecting areas from the 1950s to the 1970s. As well as individual dealers in the arches, there is a multi-dealer section in the Horse Hospital, making the Stables the perfect place for all your retro desires. The Stables were originally built and used for horses pulling barges along nearby Regent's Canal, and the 'Hospital', now a listed building, was for sick or injured horses. (Camden Market is a Saturday and Sunday market, and it is best to assume the shops are closed during the week.)

Arch 79 ARCH 79, THE STABLES, CHALK FARM ROAD, LONDON NW1 8AH
Unmistakable 50s and 60s space-age influenced plastics sit with funky lighting and chrome furniture at this Camden Stables specialist dealer. Call here for a great choice of pop style.

20th Century Decorative Arts UNIT 85 STABLES MARKET,
CHALK FARM ROAD, LONDON NW1 8AH
The best of eclectic design from the second half of the 20th century is showcased in the Bohemian setting. Think Danish and Italian modern and funky glass lighting.

Stuff 67 UNIT 67, THE CATACOMBS, CHALK FARM ROAD, LONDON NW1 8AH
Tucked behind the arches in the 'catacombs' is this dealer with a large selection of small and affordable collectibles from the 50s to the 70s.

DecoDivine UNIT 88a, THE STABLES, CHALK FARM, LONDON NW1 9AF
DecoDivine sells 20th-century furniture and decorative arts from the 1930s to the 1970s. Pieces are displayed with sophistication and are reasonably priced.

Sergio Guazzelli UNIT 88, THE STABLES, CHALK FARM ROAD, LONDON NW1 9AH ✆ 07956 645 492
Architect, interior designer and purveyor of style, Sergio Guazzelli sells furniture and lighting from the 50s to the 70s, creating a very individual look which is modernism without the minimalism.

CO2 UNIT 90, THE STABLES, CHALK FARM, LONDON NW1 9AF
www.co2moderndesign.com www.patrickbrillet.com
These specialist mid-century modern dealers have excellent examples of the style with many large and attributed pieces. From Herman Miller to Florence Knoll, the second half of the 20th century is presented with enthusiasm and expertise.

The Horse Hospital THE STABLES, CHALK FARM ROAD, LONDON NW1 9AF
This antique market has over fifty dealers in the old Horse Hospital within Stables Market. Although not specifically a mid-century modern venue, many dealers seem to follow the lead of individual shops in the Stables with a good selection of vintage design as well as glass, silver and other general antiques.

ALSO OF INTEREST

Eat My Handbag Bitch 37 DRURY LANE, COVENT GARDEN, LONDON WC2B 5RR ✆ 020 7836 0830 *www.eatmyhandbagbitch.co.uk*
Try this dealer in Italian, Scandinavian and British post-War design for a more sophisticated look than the name suggests. Clean lines of modernist furniture are brightened with cheeky objects and art. Another venue is in the lower ground floor of Selfridges on Oxford Street.

Planet Bazaar 397 ST JOHN STREET, LONDON EC1V 4LD
✆ 020 7278 7793 *www.planetbazaar.co.uk*
Describing itself as London's 'top pop shop', Planet Bazaar sells a surprising range of 20th-century design classics, including art, furniture and lifestyle accessories. Bright colours, plastics and quirky designs abound.

NoHo 68 MARYLEBONE HIGH STREET, LONDON W1U 5JH ✆ 020 7487 3009
On upmarket Marylebone High Street, you will find this sweet shop dealing in carefully selected post-War furniture and objects. The emphasis is on clean and classic lines that will blend with most interiors.

Solomon 49 PARK ROAD, LONDON N8 8SY ✆ 020 8341 1817
A recent style change at Solomon has seen him move from **Arts & Crafts** to funky 50s, 60s and 70s.

New School

Are these really antique shops, or are they merely purveyors of second-hand design classics? Who cares? They are seriously cool. The new school of 'antique' shops defies all the rules. Gone is the notion that something has to be one hundred years old to be antique. 'Proper' antiques from the 18th and 19th centuries are 'in', but only if they confront the viewer, perhaps with scale, individuality, wonderful design, beauty, irony or flair. Pieces of 1970s plastic and everything else in between are also in, and sitting next to the 'proper' antiques, provided they have the same effect. By mixing all that's been stylish and funky over the course of three centuries, the new school creates surprising and wonderful results. This is where design meets antiques. It's the cutting edge and the most exciting thing to happen in the world of antiques, possibly ever!

In a school without rules, it should be no surprise that there is not much conformity. The new school dealers each add their own individuality to their collections, so where you should visit depends on your own taste and budget. You can take clues from each store's location: **Lillie Road** will be more feminine and decorative; **King's Road** bolder and masculine; and **Pimlico Road** will have some rarer pieces.

WHERE TO GO

CHELSEA & FULHAM

297 297 LILLIE ROAD, LONDON SW6 7LL ℂ 020 7386 1888 ▶ 14

295 295 LILLIE ROAD, LONDON SW6 7LL ℂ 020 7381 5277 ▶ 14

Stephen Sprake Antiques 283 LILLIE ROAD, LONDON SW6 7LL
ℂ 020 7381 3209 ▶ 14

McWhirter 22 PARK WALK, LONDON SW10 0AQ ℂ 020 7351 5399
www.jamesmcwhirter.com ▶ 22

Core One THE GASWORKS, GATE D, 2 MICHAEL ROAD, LONDON SW6 2AN
ℂ 020 7371 5700 ▶ 31

BELGRAVIA

Blanchard 86–88 PIMLICO ROAD, LONDON SW1W 8PL ℂ 020 7823 6310 ▶ 34

Christopher Howe 93 PIMLICO ROAD, LONDON SW1W 8PH ℂ 020 7730 7987
www.howelondon.com ▶ 38

Christopher Hodsoll (including Bennison) 89–91 PIMLICO ROAD,
LONDON SW1W 8PH ℂ 020 7730 3370 www.hodsoll.com ▶ 38

Lamberty Antiques 46 PIMLICO ROAD, LONDON SW1W 8LP ℂ 020 7823 5115
www.lamberty.co.uk ▶ 38

Humphrey Carrasco 43 PIMLICO ROAD, LONDON SW1W 8NE
© 020 7730 9911 ▶ 38

MARYLEBONE

Marchand 14 CHURCH STREET, LONDON NW8 8EP © 020 7724 9238 ▶ 79

Bloch Antiques 22 CHURCH STREET, LONDON NW8 8EP
© 020 7723 6575 ▶ 79

Andrew Nebbett Antiques 35–37 CHURCH STREET, LONDON NW8 8ES
© 020 7723 2303 *www.andrewnebbett.com* ▶ 79

BATTERSEA

Daniel Mankowitz STUDIO F1, THE IMPERIAL LAUNDRY,
71 WARRINER GARDENS, LONDON SW11 4XW
© 020 7498 0000 *www.danielmankowitz.com*
Here you will encounter the bold and traditional, the eclectic and unusual, and the
contemporary and chic. Basically, if it is stimulating, imposing or well designed, Danny
will display and sell it with flair.

From bus stop 'G' at South Kensington station, take the 345 bus to the Latchmere in
Battersea. Walk east on Battersea Park Road until Beechmore Road where you turn
left. Your first right is Warriner Gardens, and you will see the Imperial Laundry.

RUSTIC AND FOLK ART

The term folk art covers a variety of styles. These styles are generally associated with traditions and characteristics of local culture, often primitive, and are (or were) generally produced by artisans without formal or academic training.

In provincial England, folk art could be a Windsor chair, whereas in Germany it could refer to a Black Forest carving. In France, folk art is called *art populaire* and is often made of items taken from nature such as twigs, roots, branches and antlers. In the United States there is Adirondack or cowboy art. Finally, there is tramp art, which refers to objects made from disused cigar boxes chipped in a zigzag shape and layered in geometric pattern. Tramp art was made across Europe and the USA from the mid-19th century until the Great Depression. All these forms of rustic art are increasingly collectible and may be incorporated in modern and/or eclectic interiors. As a cosmopolitan city, London is not particularly known for its country furniture but has a great selection of all forms of folk art.

WHERE TO GO

MARYLEBONE

Magus 4 CHURCH STREET, LONDON NW8 8ED ℰ 020 7724 1278 ▶ 75

Tara 6 CHURCH STREET, LONDON NW8 8ED ℰ 020 7724 2405 ▶ 75

North West Eight 36 CHURCH STREET, LONDON NW8 8EP
ℰ 020 7723 9337 ▶ 79

Raffles 40 CHURCH STREET, LONDON NW8 8EP ℰ 020 7724 6384 ▶ 80

Patricia Harvey Antiques and Decoration 42 CHURCH STREET,
LONDON NW8 8EP ℰ 020 7262 8989 *www.patriciaharveyantiques.co.uk* ▶ 80

ISLINGTON

Kate Bannister 118 ISLINGTON HIGH STREET, LONDON N1 8EG ▶ 86

Matthew Austin-Cooper 118 ISLINGTON HIGH STREET, LONDON N1 8EG ▶ 86

BATTERSEA

Robert Young Antiques 68 BATTERSEA BRIDGE ROAD, LONDON SW11 3AG
ℰ 020 7228 7847 *www.robertyoungantiques.com*
You would not believe what lies behind the door of 68 Battersea Bridge Road. This is one of the most charming and intimate galleries devoted to folk art. Here you will discover painted and naive furniture and objects of the highest quality and rarity. To get there either take a taxi or the tube to South Kensington (District, Circle and Piccadilly lines) station and then take the 345 bus from bus stop 'G' outside the station.

Relic 127 PANCRAS ROAD, LONDON NW1 1UN
℗ 020 7485 7810 *www.rubylane.com/shops/relic*
Decorative antique offerings with something for everyone are on offer at this by-appointment warehouse. Relic is a veritable treasure trove of French painted, rustic, country, *art populaire* and fairground furniture and decorative objects. (If you are moving on to the South of France, ask Malcolm about his B&B in Clermont L'Herault, a popular haunt of London's decorative dealers during trade fairs in the region.)

FOR SERIOUS BUYERS

Warner Daly ℗ 020 8333 5583
An independent London dealer without an official shop, Warner often has pieces of rustic charm and eclectic wackiness available at competitive prices.

Jay Arenski (℗ 020 8202 3075) **and Peter Petrou** (℗ 07831 633 886)
www.arenski.com and *www.peterpetrou.com*
Although not solely dealers in rustic art and antiques, Arenski and Petrou are highly acclaimed for their quality offerings of Black Forest, colonial furniture, antiquities, Grand Tour objects and even 1960s decorative arts. For the most interesting and the widest range of antique offerings in London call for an appointment.

SALVAGE STYLE

The term 'architectural salvage' covers any element of a building which has been removed, usually during the building's renovation or demolition. It includes a myriad of items such as doors, stained glass, baths, basins, reclaimed floors, radiators and door hardware. Depending on its quality and rarity, salvage can range in price from a fraction of the cost of buying new to many multiples thereof. Regardless of price, salvage can give character and add a touch of class to a new building.

London salvage yards fall into two categories. First there are general salvage dealers who take in almost all materials, regardless of age or importance, and store the pieces in large indoor and/or outdoor areas. At these yards, salvage is sold 'as is'. The yard has not and will not restore items for sale. This is the gritty wholesale end of the business. Searching for your desired pieces requires hard work and patience. However, this is where you are most likely to find bargains – buried in a sea of salvage.

The other type of architectural salvage yard is at the higher end of the business. Items are generally selected for their interest and value. The salvage, ranging up to museum-quality pieces, is usually presented in a clean, approachable manner. These dealers have sometimes restored pieces or will carry out restoration. You will pay more, but you won't have to spend hours sifting through mountains of material.

FIVE TIPS FOR BUYING SALVAGE

1. Wear practical clothes and shoes. You will get dirty at all but the most upmarket yards.

2. Check doors, windows and other elements for signs of warping which will make fitting the element a nightmare.

3. If wood or metal has been stripped by dipping it in acid, look for glue or putty, particularly in the joints, which may have been weakened by the process.

4. Remember that old English taps and other bathroom fittings may not connect to those in modern homes without specialist refitting.

5. Remember to bring a tape measure, pen and paper.

WHERE TO GO

This section of the guide focuses on selective, higher-end salvage yards. For comprehensive listings including general salvage log on to *www.salvo.co.uk*.

FULHAM

Architectural Antiques 312 LILLIE ROAD, LONDON SW6 7PS
✆ 020 7385 3519   ▶ 13

Townsends 81 ABBEY ROAD, LONDON NW8 0AE 📞 020 7624 4756

Off the beaten track but in the exceedingly smart neighbourhood of St John's Wood, Townsends has two venues. The Abbey Road shop sells a selection of reproduction and period fireplaces. Five minutes' walk away, the large warehouse at 96a Clifton Hill has 10,000 square feet of fireplaces, fenders, grates and firedogs. Everything is clean and neatly presented with a particular strength in turn-of-the-century **Arts & Crafts** and **Art Nouveau** fireplaces. As well as fireplaces, you will find mirrors, picture frames, gates and stained glass. There is definitely an eye for quality and design at this beautiful salvage shop.

By tube, go to St John's Wood (Jubilee line) station and walk north on Finchley Road. Turn left on Marlborough Place and then right on Abbey Road. Clifton Road will be the third street on your left, and the main showroom is a block beyond that.

SHOREDITCH

LASSCO and Westland & Co. ST MICHAEL'S CHURCH, MARK STREET
(OFF PAUL STREET), LONDON EC2A 4ER 📞 020 7749 9944 *www.lassco.co.uk*
AND 📞 020 7739 8094 *www.westland.co.uk*

The several branches of LASSCO form London's premier architectural salvage dealers. At St Michael's, LASSCO shares a church conversion with Westland. Together the two companies have a huge stock salvaged from impressive period properties throughout Europe. This is the place to come if you desire a completely panelled room, a 17th-century fireplace or the remnants of a Baroque garden to create your own mini-Versailles. There is also a large selection of brass hardware. Much of the stock is absolutely magnificent and prices can run into tens of thousands. Whatever your budget, however, a visit is definitely worth your while in order to develop ideas and see the old church setting. You will find more affordable pieces mixed in with the fabulous.

Take the tube to Old Street (Northern line). You must take exit 4 to the east side of City Road South and walk until you see Leonard Street, where you will turn left. Walk past Tabernacle Street and Saint Paul Street, and LASSCO will be on your right.

Renaissance 193–195 CITY ROAD, LONDON EC1V 1JN
📞 020 7251 8844 *www.renaissancelondon.com*

Roughly opposite Moorfields Eye Hospital on City Road, Renaissance is about two thirds of a mile/one kilometre from LASSCO St Michael's. It specializes in salvaged and reproduction fireplaces in all materials and styles. It also has a selection of doors, radiators and other interesting architectural elements.

HAMMERSMITH

Stamford Brook Architectural Antiques 351 KING STREET,
LONDON W6 2NH 📞 020 8741 7883 *www.aa-fireplaces.co.uk*

This gem of a shop specializes in marble fireplaces, with literally hundreds from which to choose. There is also a large and ever-changing selection of other antiques such as mirrors, frames, metalwork and lighting, all with impressive style, reasonable prices and friendly service.

To get there by tube, take the Ealing Broadway or Richmond branch of the District line to Ravenscourt Park station. Turn left out of the station and then take a quick right on to King Street. The yard will then be about 200 yards/180 metres ahead of you on the other side of King Street.

SOUTHWARK

LASSCO Warehouse   41 MALTBY STREET, LONDON SE1 3PA
℗ 020 7394 2101 *www.lassco.co.uk*
This branch of LASSCO has a wider range of periods, styles and prices than LASSCO St Michael's. At the same location, you will also find LASSCO RBK (Radiators, Bathrooms and Kitchens) with an enormous selection of period items, many of which have been refurbished. The warehouse will have hundreds of doors, lights, architectural mouldings, elements and period hardware. You can also buy garden elements and reclaimed flooring at the Maltby Street premises.

The best way to get to LASSCO Warehouse is by taxi. Otherwise, by tube, take the City branch of the Northern line to London Bridge station. Exit the station on to Tooley Street and turn right towards Tower Bridge. Keep walking for ten minutes until you hit Tower Bridge Road, at which point you turn right. Walk under the railway bridge and turn left on to Tanner Street (by the Raven in the Tower pub). This leads you on to Maltby Street and LASSCO.

GREENWICH

Lamont Antiques   UNIT K, TUNNEL AVENUE TRADING ESTATE,
LONDON SE10 0QH ℗ 020 8305 2230
This antique and architectural salvage dealer is definitely off the beaten track. You will understand why it has to be that way when you enter the massive warehouse, which is packed on two levels with furniture, stained glass, church and pub fittings, panelled rooms, period mouldings and stone fragments. Lamont needs a lot of space to display its offerings from dozens, if not hundreds, of buildings throughout Britain.

To get there by public transport, take the Jubilee line tube to North Greenwich station. From there, it will take you 10 to 15 minutes through an industrial wasteland to get to Lamont on foot, so a taxi is definitely recommended!

Shabby Chic/
Painted French

Shabby chic was introduced as a style in the 1980s by British designer Rachel Ashwell. The phrase refers to a comfortable interior style, in a soft colour palette, where aesthetics, comfort and usability are all important. Antique and vintage furniture is usually painted in soft colours (often white), and the original style covered much of this with overstuffed slipcovers. Painted wood is often distressed, either after recent restoration or as the authentic result of wear and tear over time. Any minor knocks or scratches will usually add to the distressed look.

While shabby chic's basic tenets remain ever popular, the focus has moved from overstuffing, slip covers and chintzes to eclecticism. People are more likely to describe the look as 'decorative' or 'vintage', and at a stretch these terms can be used to describe individual sub-genres. With the decorative look, antiques, second-hand objects and new pieces are mixed in a way that is interesting and personal to create a playful and stylish interior. The vintage style maintains a tendency to display collections, from crowns to tea caddies or even less valuable items such as 1920s biscuit tins.

In either case, architectural fragments are often incorporated into designs in which every piece is selected for aesthetic appeal and has a story to tell. Great value is not placed on purity or absolute authenticity, and pieces do not have to be expensive. The shabby chic look may be assembled on a shoe-string budget by attending fleamarkets and antique fairs and scouring small antique shops. Also, if you are trying to collect items of a more pure nature, you may wish to mix in a few shabby chic items to soften the look and convey an enthusiasm for all that is old.

The **Lillie Road** (together with the cache of shops at the SW6 end of **Fulham Road**) and **Church Street** are the best streets in London for picking up inexpensive treasures and the soft, distressed French pieces which blend so well. There are also several dealers to visit in **Camden Passage**. Prices will vary depending on the authenticity of the object, but if you are looking for comfortable pieces with a distressed look, you will not be disappointed.

WHERE TO GO

FULHAM

291 Decorative Antiques 291 LILLIE ROAD, LONDON SW6 7LL
☎ 020 7381 5008 ▶ 14

Andrew Bewick 287 LILLIE ROAD, LONDON SW6 7LL ☎ 020 7385 9025 ▶ 14

Decorative Antiques 284 LILLIE ROAD, LONDON SW6 7PX
☎ 020 7610 2694 ▶ 14

Nimmo & Spooner 277 LILLIE ROAD, LONDON SW6 7LL
☎ 020 7385 2724 ▶ 14

Artefact 273 LILLIE ROAD, LONDON SW6 7LL © 020 7381 2500 ▶ 16

Mark Maynard Antiques 651 FULHAM ROAD/2A CASSIDY ROAD, LONDON SW6 5PU © 020 7731 3533 ▶ 22

Judy Greenwood Antiques 657–659 FULHAM ROAD, LONDON SW6 5PY © 020 7736 6037 ▶ 22

CHELSEA

M. Charpentier Antiques 498 KING'S ROAD, LONDON SW10 0LE © 020 7351 1442 ▶ 27

Decorative Living 55 NEW KING'S ROAD, LONDON SW6 4SE © 020 7736 5623 ▶ 32

BELGRAVIA

Appley Hoare Antiques 30 PIMLICO ROAD, LONDON SW1W 8LJ © 020 7730 7070 *www.appleyhoare.com* ▶ 39

MARYLEBONE

Marchand 14 CHURCH STREET, LONDON NW8 8EP © 020 7724 9238 ▶ 79

North West Eight 36 CHURCH STREET, LONDON NW8 8EP © 020 7723 9337 ▶ 79

Victoria Harvey at Deuxieme 44 CHURCH STREET, LONDON NW8 8EP © 020 7724 0738 ▶ 80

ISLINGTON

Max-Oliver 108 ISLINGTON HIGH STREET, LONDON N1 8EG © 020 7354 0777 *www.max-oliver.co.uk* ▶ 86

Rosemary Conquest 27 CAMDEN PASSAGE, LONDON N1 8EA © 020 7359 0616 *www.rosemaryconquest.com* ▶ 89

CROUCH END

Andrew Sorrell FLORAL HALL, CROUCH HILL, LONDON N8 9DX © 020 8348 7309
This friendly neighbourhood dealer runs a pretty corner antique shop from his father's original florist shop. The look is all softness and prettiness with peeling paint, chandeliers and country French furniture and objects with a few pieces of English furniture mixed in for good measure. The turnover is fast and the prices are very competitive. Highly recommended. (By the time you make it, you will need a stop at the World Café across the road where you can relax with the local, liberal 'loiterati'. To get there by public transport from Euston station bus stop 'C', take the number 91 bus to Crouch End Broadway.

CLAPHAM

Josephine Ryan   63 ABBEVILLE ROAD, LONDON SW4 9JW   © 020 8675 3900
Delicate and fanciful antiques are complemented by garden statuary, architectural fragments and exquisite curiosities at Clapham's version of **Lillie Road**. With a definite feminine touch, this shop sells all that is soft, gorgeous and beautiful with mostly French painted furniture, whimsical accessories and elegant chandeliers. To get there, take the Northern line to Clapham South station and walk for about 10 to 15 minutes along Clapham Common South Side (street) to Narbonne Street. Turn right, and you will soon see Abbeville Road and Josephine Ryan's gem of a shop.

BARNES

Tobias and the Angel   68 WHITE HART LANE,
LONDON SW13 0PZ   © 020 8296 0058
This Barnes staple has a mood and personality all of its own. There are country and painted pieces of furniture, all of which have age and an air of comfort and softness. The shop also sells a range of more modern homewares and linens to complement the look. By public transport from Hammersmith (Hammersmith & City, Piccadilly and District lines) station take the 209 bus from stop 'C' to the corner of Mortlake High Street and White Hart Lane. You will find the store opposite the intersection of White Hart Lane and Archway Street.

6 Tips and Tricks

RESTORATION

If a piece needs restoration, you may find it easier (and less expensive) to have this done in England. The standard of restoration in England is very high, especially in London. The best way to find a restorer is to ask the dealer from whom you are purchasing the piece to have it restored for you using his or her personal restorers.

Alternatively, the British Antique Furniture Restorers' Association (B.A.F.R.A.) is a good organization to contact. On its website (*www.bafra.org.uk*) you will be able to find restorers, conservators and useful articles.

VAT RULES

When asking for the best price from a dealer, always be sure to tell him or her if you will be exporting your purchases from the United Kingdom. Under UK VAT rules, VAT registered dealers (i.e. most if not all full-time dealers) have to pay 17.5% VAT on their profit if the piece is sold within the UK. If the piece is for export, however, no VAT is due, so the dealer will be able to offer you a lower price and make the same profit.

EXPORT RULES

Buying antiques for export is reasonably straightforward. The rules regarding export are as follows:

▪ Most objects that fall under the £65,000 threshold and are exported from Britain to Europe do not require an export licence (although there are exceptions in some categories, most notably British portraits, manuscripts, photographs, archaeological pieces and paintings).

▪ Any object being exported outside Europe and worth more than £30,400 requires an export licence which can usually be obtained through the dealer or shipper.

The Department for Culture, Media and Sport, Export Licensing Unit

2–4 COCKSPUR STREET, LONDON SW1Y 5DH ✆ 020 7211 6200

▪ If an item contains endangered species of floral or fauna (this includes ivory), then the piece must be antique and have a C.I.T.E.S. (Convention on International Trade in Endangered Species) certificate obtained from C.I.T.E.S.

Licensing, Department for Environment, Food and Rural Affairs

FLOOR 1, ZONE 17, TEMPLE QUAY HOUSE, 2 THE SQUARE,
TEMPLE QUAY, BRISTOL BS1 6EB ✆ 0117 372 8168 *www.ukcites.gov.uk*

▪ If you are exporting antiques to the United States, all wooden furniture is duty-free regardless of age. Any other antique must be over one hundred years old to be exempt from US import duty. A reputable dealer will provide you with an invoice which specifically states if the piece is over one hundred years old.

▪ If you are exporting to Australia, Goods & Service Tax (GST) of 10% is payable in Australia on all goods irrespective of what they are and whether they would normally attract a tax.

▪ All goods entering Canada are subject to Goods & Service Tax (GST) of 7% if they are subsequently sold on.

▪ There is generally no duty on antique/second-hand furniture imported to Japan, but there is a 5% consumption tax. You will need to liaise with your shippers to arrange photographs of the pieces in the shipment for customs.

Shipping

If you plan to buy anything too big to take home in your luggage, you will need to have a shipper. The cost of shipping goods to another country varies greatly depending on how much you buy.

If you are buying just a few modestly priced pieces, it can be almost prohibitively expensive, costing as much as – if not more than – your purchase. A good rule of thumb is to allow about £300 for shipping a single, medium-sized piece of furniture (such as a table) to the United States. As you add more pieces, the per unit cost should come down.

If you are buying many pieces, it may be more economical to ship a whole container. Containers come in either 20 or 40 foot lengths. When you are buying this quantity, a good rule of thumb is to estimate your shipping cost to be between 15% and 20% of the cost of the items shipped. Two factors which will affect the price are the number of collection points the shippers need to visit in order to pick up your purchases and the value of your goods for insurance purposes.

If you are buying in this quantity, most shippers will give you a 'buying kit'. This includes a notebook for you to list all the relevant information about your purchases. You will then label each of your purchases with a tag or sticker provided by the shipper and leave it with the dealer. After you give your list of purchases to the shippers, they will collect and ship all of your pieces to you.

There are two ways to ship: by sea or by air. Sea is the cheaper option if the destination is near a port, such as New York, and a delivery to America takes about 6–8 weeks from the time of collection. Air shipping often takes one or two days and may well cost less if the destination is inland, such as Chicago. It can be worth comparing the price of two forms of shipping.

As paying dealers in foreign currency can be a challenge, a service that many shippers offer is to set up a client account whereby you forward a single payment to the shipper (an estimate of the amount which you think will cover all of your purchases). When you make purchases, you can tell the dealer that the shippers will pay on your behalf when they collect.

USEFUL SHIPPING ADDRESSES

Anglo Pacific (Fine Art)
Units 1 & 2,
Bush Industrial Estate,
Standard Road,
London NW10 6DF
☏ 020 8965 1234
www.anglopacific.co.uk

B. B. F. Shipping
Unit 12, North Crescent,
London E16 4TG
☏ 020 7511 6107

Constantine Limited
134 Queens Road,
London SE15 2HR
☏ 020 7732 8123

Gander & White Shipping
Unit 1,
St Martin's Way,
London SW17 0JH
☏ 020 8971 7171
www.ganderandwhite.com

Hedleys Humpers
3 St Leonards Road,
London NW10 6SX
☏ 020 8965 8733
www.hedleyshumpers.com

Kuwahara
6 McNicol Drive,
London NW10 7AW
☏ 020 8963 1100
www.kuwahara.co.uk

Lockson Services
Unit 1, Heath Park
Industrial Estate,
Freshwater Road,
Chadwell Heath,
Essex RM8 1RX
☏ 020 8597 2889
www.lockson.co.uk

Stephen Morris Shipping
Brent Trading Estate,
390 North Circular Road,
London NW10 0JF
☏ 020 8830 1919
www.stemo.co.uk

Nelson Shipping
Unit C3, Six Bridges
Trading Estate,
Marlborough Grove,
London SE1 5JT
☏ 020 7394 7770

Nippon Express (U.K.)
(Japan/Far East specialist)
Unit 7, Parkway Trading
Estate, Cranford Lane,
Heston, Hounslow,
Middlesex TW5 9NE
☏ 020 8737 4000
www.nipponexpress.net

The Packing Shop
6–12 Ponton Road,
London SW8 5BA
☏ 020 7498 3255

PDQ Freight (Art Move)
Unit 4, Court 1,
Challenge Road,
Ashford, Middlesex
TW15 1AX
☏ 01784 243 695
www.pdq.uk.com

Robert Boys Shipping
Unit D, Tunnel Avenue
Trading Estate,
Tunnel Avenue, Greenwich,
London SE10 0QH
☏ 020 8858 3355

L. J. Roberton
Mallard House,
402 Roding Lane South,
Woodford Green,
Essex IG8 8EY
☏ 020 8551 8999

Seabourne Mailpack Worldwide
Unit 13,
Saxon Way,
West Drayton,
Middlesex UB7 0LW
☏ 020 8897 3888
www.seabourne-mailpack.com

Trans Euro Worldwide Movers
Drury Way, Brent Park,
London NW10 0JN
☏ 020 8784 0100

REFERENCE MATERIAL

There are many books about antiques and authenticity, but they vary a great deal in terms of quality. Below is a list of recommended titles for those wishing to expand their knowledge.

Antique Furniture Expert: How You Can Identify, Date and Authenticate by Peter Philip and Gillian Walkling with consultant editor John Bly

English Furniture: The Georgian Period (1750–1830) by F. Rose and Margaret Jourdain (the revered high priestess of English furniture)

Georgian Cabinet-Makers, c. 1700–1800 by Ralph Edwards

History of English Furniture: Age of Mahogany by Percy Macquoid

History of English Furniture: Age of Oak by Percy Macquoid

History of English Furniture: Age of Satinwood by Percy Macquoid

History of English Furniture: Age of Walnut by Percy Macquoid

Regency Furniture 1795–1830 by Margaret Jourdain

The Shorter Dictionary of English Furniture by Ralph Edwards and Percy Macquoid

POSTCODES

Here is an example of how London postcodes work. The postcode for Preston Fitzgerald Antiques is NW8 8EE. The first two letters tell you that the shop is north-west of central London. The first number in the postcode generally gives an indication of proximity to central London. However, it does not follow that NW8 is eight times further from the centre than NW1. Postcodes in which the second letter is 'C' (for 'central') refer to addresses within the City of London business district or the West End. Preston Fitzgerald will share the whole postcode NW8 8EE with no more than a dozen or so addresses.

Free websites such as *www.streetmap.co.uk* and *www.multimap.com* use this information to produce maps which can mark the location of a postcode with great accuracy. The journey planner at *www.tfl.gov.uk* also uses the same information to produce point-to-point directions between locations by public transport.

7 Quick Guide

This Quick Guide shows price ranges by area and highlights the key periods in both English and French history. The price guide follows the same order as Street-by-Street and gives rough estimates of the number of dealers in any one location, as well as giving you an idea of whether the emphasis of the dealers on the street tends to be fine or decorative quality.

Area	Strength (out of 10)		Number of Dealers	Price
	Decorative Antiques	Fine Antiques		
Lillie Road	10	2	20	£200–10,000
Fulham Road sw10 & sw6	7	5	<10	£100–10,000
Fulham Road sw3	7	10	15–20	£2,000–500,000
King's Road	10	7	50+	£200–50,000
Pimlico Road	10	8	34	£1,000–100,000
St James's	5	10	10	£2,000–100,000
Mayfair	5	10	50+	£5,000–1,000,000
Kensington Church Street	5	9	65	£500–100,000
Notting Hill	8	5	100+	£50–10,000
Church Street	8	6	100+	£50–10,000
Camden Passage	8	5	100+	£50–10,000

TIMELINES

Dates	Monarch	Style
1660–85	Charles II	Baroque / Restoration
1685–88	James II	
1689–1702	William and Mary	
1702–14	Anne	Queen Anne / Early Georgian
1714–27	George I	
1727–60	George II	English Rococo / Chippendale
1760–1820	George III	Neo-Classical / Regency
1820–30	George IV	Regency / George IV
1830–37	William IV	Revivalism, Eclecticism, Gothic revival, Arts & Crafts (from 1851)
1837–1901	Queen Victoria	
1901–10	Edward VII	Revivalism/Arts & Crafts

FRANCE

Dates	Monarch	Style
1643–1715	Louis XIV	Baroque
1715–74	Louis XV	Rococo / Neo-Classical
1774–92	Louis XVI	Neo-Classical
1792–99	National Convention and Directory	Directoire
1799–1815	Napoleon Bonaparte	Empire
1815–24	Louis XVIII	Restauration
1824–30	Charles X	Charles X
1830–48	Louis Philippe	Louis Philippe
1848–52	Louis Napoleon Bonaparte	Second Empire
1852–70	Napoleon III	

TOP TEN TIPS

1. Only Buy What You Like
What's the point of owning something you don't like?

2. Always Compare
When looking at a piece, determine if you have seen anything similar before. Decide what you think the date might be.

3. Determine the Materials and Construction
Look at how the piece is made and the materials. Do the materials and construction method make sense when considering the purported date of the piece?

4. Ask Yourself 'Is it Quality?'
Determine if the piece is of good quality. Are the joints well made? Is the wood of good quality? Is the gilt really gold?

5. Look for Good Patina
When judging patina, you should look for even, natural wear from use, a slight build-up of dirt and wax in the indented areas and an evenness to the grain of the wood. Ideally, the best wood should also have a rich colour with a highly figured grain.

6. Look for Signs of Use
Look for the all telling signs of age. Are there knocks on the feet? Does the wood show marks of normal use? If an 'antique' looks brand new, it probably is.

7. Check for Restorations and Alterations
Has the piece been repolished, cut down, reveneered or given new handles? Is the piece a marriage? (That is, has it been made up from two or more original, but different, pieces?)

8. Ask Questions
You may be quite surprised at how much you are told about any provenance or recent restoration.

9. Get a Written Bill of Sale
This is important for recording when, where and for how much you acquired the piece. It will help when it comes to insuring or selling the piece.

10. You Will Make Mistakes
Even the best dealers make mistakes, but you will learn from mistakes much faster than from books. So long as you begin with rule number one, you won't go too far wrong.

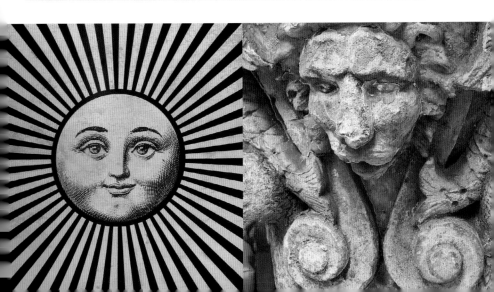

GLOSSARY

Aesthetic A late 19th-century English and American artistic movement with the basic principle of 'art for art's sake'. Forms and motifs derive from Japanese art and design.

Arcade A lane or passage with a roof and individual shops on either side.

Architectural Salvage Any kind of architectural feature or decoration taken from a demolished or renovated building.

Art Deco An inter-war style with a modern and anti-historical outlook which utilized mechanization and streamlined forms.

Art Nouveau A decorative style at the height of popularity in around 1900 which utilized naturalistic forms, particularly plant tendrils, 'whiplash' curves and the femme fatale.

Art Populaire The French name for a **folk art** which is unified by the creator's lack of formal training and is often made from found materials in unconstrained forms.

Art Pottery Pottery created by a studio potter (someone who works in a traditional manner as opposed to a factory). The common theme in studio pottery is the artistic creation and individuality.

Attributed This phrase implies that there is an academic or research-based reason to assume a piece was made by a particular artist or craftsman. However, the attribution is only an opinion and may be disputed.

Aubusson A carpet from the 18th century. It has a smooth-faced woven knot, made in Louis XVI and Empire styles with symmetrical designs and classical motifs in soft colours.

BADA The British Antique Dealers' Association (BADA) is the trade association for the leading antique dealers in Britain. Since its foundation in 1918, BADA has set the standard for trading in the antiques business (see *www.bada.org*).

Black Forest Objects of carved wood in the form of animals, cuckoo-clocks, bears or rabbits made in Germany and Switzerland near the Black Forest region in the 19th and early 20th centuries.

Brocante A French term for second-hand goods, usually bought at a flea market. Some dealers joke that brocante is French for junk.

Brown A trade phrase describing furniture that is not painted, gilt or otherwise decorated, usually implying that it is **Georgian**, wooden furniture.

Cabriole Leg An 18th-century style of leg which curves out at the knee and is carved and tapered in towards the foot. The foot is usually in the shape of a bun, hoof, scroll or ball-and-claw.

Ceramic A general phrase that covers all pottery and porcelain.

Chippendale An English mid-18th-century cabinetmaker of the highest standard, Chippendale created and spread the English Rococo style through publishing the design books, *The Gentleman & Cabinet Maker's Director* (1754, 1755 and 1762).

Collectibles Objects which are collected, usually implying genres such as kitchenalia, toys, ceramics, glass and more modern decorative arts.

Conservator A craftsman who preserves an antique's condition from further decline, as opposed to a restorer who returns a piece to a condition that is as close as possible to its original state.

Dateline A term used when an antique fair has a latest possible date from which antiques can still be included in the fair. This usually implies that the fair is vetted for the dateline as well.

Decorative A trade phrase implying that a piece is more valuable for its decorative use than its artistic purity.

Decorative Arts All the arts which are not fine arts, i.e. not painting, sculpture and architecture.

Delft A Dutch town which created tin-glazed earthenware in the 17th century in the Chinese style, also used to describe tin-glazed earthenware produced in Germany and England.

Earthenware Pottery (all wares made from baked clay).

Edwardian The period in Britain during King Edward VII's reign (1901–10). Decorative arts from this period are often in revivalist styles.

Empire The period between 1799 and 1815 when Napoleon ruled France and coincided with a late Neo-Classical style of bold antique forms, usually created out of one material (often mahogany mounted with ormolu). The style spread through Europe with Napoleon's armies.

Export Porcelain ('Export') Porcelain made in China for export to other parts of the world, including the Middle East, Europe and the United States.

Faience The French term for tin-glazed earthenware. The tin glaze gives a white background colour. *Faenza* is the Italian term for faience.

Famille Verte A category of 17th-century Chinese porcelain which is decorated in the overglazed enamel colours of green and iron-red.

Folk Art Art and antiques created by artists lacking formal training, generally thought to reflect the traditions and characteristics of the local culture.

French Country/Provincial The style of the French provinces in the 17th and 18th centuries. Pieces are often made of fruitwood with curving shapes and simple carving.

Gardenalia A term used to classify all antique things for and from the garden.

Georgian The period in Britain from 1714 to 1830 during which the Kings were George I, George II, George III and George IV. The styles included during this period are Baroque, Rococo and Neo-Classical.

Giltwood Wood that has literally been decorated with gold leaf.

Gothic Revival Refers to a stylistic movement in both the 18th and 19th centuries, when architecture and decorative arts were made in a concertedly revivalist style of medieval Gothic.

Grand Tour An extended tour of Europe, particularly Italy, which was part of the education of upper-class English men during the 18th century.

Imperial Chinese arts made for the Emperor or for use at the palace.

Iznik Earthenware from the 15th and 16th centuries, made in what is present-day Turkey, with a white slip and decorated in blue, black and green.

Japanned A decorative technique which imitates oriental lacquer.

Knock It Out A term used in the antiques trade to imply that the dealer is willing to make a small profit in order to obtain a quick sale.

Kunstkammer Literally an 'art cabinet' – a cabinet from the 16th century which had many compartments in which the collector would house art objects and curiosities.

LAPADA The Association of Art & Antique Dealers which is the largest trade association in Britain (*www.lapada.co.uk*).

Mahogany A dark, close-grained wood from the Americas and West Indies, first imported to England towards the middle of the 18th century.

Majolica Tin-glazed earthenware made in the 19th and early 20th centuries in Britain and France to imitate Italian maiolica (tin-glazed earthenware from the 15th and 16th centuries).

Modernism A style of architecture and furniture in the 1920s and 1930s which was forward-looking as opposed to traditional, utilizing forms and styling from mechanization. It is similar to **Art Deco**.

Moghul Decorative arts in India during the Muslim rule of the 16th and 17th centuries.

Morris, William An English 19th-century designer and craftsman and leading proponent of the **Arts & Crafts** movement.

Neo-Classical An 18th- and 19th-century artistic movement based on ancient Greek and Roman decorative motifs. It is a formal and geometric style.

Netsuke A Japanese toggle carved in the form of a small figure which is used to fasten a purse to a cord suspended from a sash.

Objets De Vertu An English term for silver, porcelain and glass objects valued for their artistic merit.

Ormolu An English phrase for the French term *bronze doré d'or moulu*, meaning bronze gilded with ground gold.

Patina The effect of oxidation on bronze, also used to describe the texture and colour of the surface of furniture and silver.

Period A trade term which implies that a piece dates from a certain period. It usually means 18th century, i.e. a Chippendale revival chair is out of period.

Porcelain A white ceramic material which is translucent and impermeable, made from kaolin(china clay) and petunse (china stone).

Pottery All items made of baked clay.

Queen Anne The reign of Queen Anne of England from 1702 to 1714 coincided with an elegant and simplified style in all the decorative arts, particularly furniture and silver. In furniture, the use of walnut, cabriole legs and interesting veneers were characteristic features.

Quimper Faience pottery from Brittany which is decorated in high temperature colours.

Regency The period between 1811 and 1820 when George IV was Prince Regent. It is also an imprecise term to describe British furniture and objects in the Neo-Classical style from about 1790 until 1840.

Restorer A craftsman who brings antiques (paintings, furniture, objects etc.) back to their original condition.

Revival A piece that is of a later date than the style initially suggests. Revivals are not modern reproductions and are usually Victorian or Edwardian.

Runner An antique dealer without a shop, who often buys in the country and sells quickly to dealers with shops.

Rustic Folk art made from natural materials such as twigs, roots, branches and antlers. This is often also called Adirondack or cowboy art in America.

Sampler An embroidered panel displaying various types of stitches, often made by young women as a demonstration of their skills. A sampler often features letters of the alphabet or pious phrases.

Sconce A wall-light with a candlestick and a back of either polished metal or mirror.

Shagreen Shark or fish-skin leathers used on small boxes from the 18th century and on **Art Deco** furniture.

Signed When used in the context of furniture, it means that a piece is marked with the name of the maker, often in the form of a stamp or applied label. Much of 18th-century French furniture is signed due to guild requirements.

Smalls Refers to small and often collectible antiques such as porcelain and silver.

Staffordshire Pottery and porcelain from the 19th century made in Staffordshire, particularly the Five Towns of Burslem, Stoke, Hanley, Turnstall and Longton.

Stumpwork English 17th-century needlework depicting scenes in which most of the decoration is in raised relief on a background of wool or cotton-wool.

'Style Of' A term which means that the style looks like the style of a particular date. Often this term means that the piece is later than the style would at first suggest – thus out of period.

Tole Painted metal, often japanned.

Trade/Trade Price Someone who is a dealer, and thus a 'trader'. A trade price is a discounted price which is made in consideration that the piece will be resold at a profit.

Tramp Art Furniture and objects made from disused cigar boxes chipped in a zigzag shape and layered to create a geometric object.

Venetian Mirror A style of mirror made from the late 19th century through to modern day with pieces of cut and etched glass framing a single mirror plate.

Vet When a group of knowledgeable dealers assess the authenticity and correctness of the labels of all the antiques and paintings at a fair 'throwing off', i.e. denying entry, to any object that is not completely authentic or correctly labelled.

Victorian The period in Britain during Queen Victoria's reign (1837–1901). Decorative arts tend to be in flamboyant, robust and revivalist styles.

Vintage A term used to imply that a piece has age, but it is probably not antique. It is also used to imply a classic design or style.

Walnut A hard wood indigenous to Europe with a fine figure and highly prized in furniture from the 16th to 18th centuries. In England, walnut was the most valued wood until it was replaced by imported mahogany from about the 1730s.

Credits and Index

Thank you to all the dealers who allowed me to photograph their pieces and shops. All photos are credited clockwise from top left on each page. Numbers in brackets refer to the order of the illustrations on a page (i.e. 1 refers to image 1).

Credits

St John's Wood

MARYLEBONE

▶ 74

WELLINGTON ROAD

St John's Wood Road

Edgware Road

Marylebone Road

PADDINGTON

WESTBOURNE
GREEN

BAYSWATER

Sussex Gardens

Edgware Road

▲ 4   ▶ 65

NOTTING HILL

Bayswater Road

Bayswater Road

Westway

Holland Park Avenue

▶ 53

⑩

KENSINGTON

SOUTH
KENSINGTON

Holland Road

Warwick Gardens

Cromwell Road

⑩ ⑧

EARLS
COURT

▶ 12

Earls Court Road

Warwick Road

Redcliffe Gardens

Finborough Road

WEST
BROMPTON

⑪ Sunbury
15 miles/ 24 km

⑥ Criterion
Riverside
Auctions

①

MAYFAIR

⑥   ▶ 46

Park Lane

Knightsbridge

Grosvenor Place

②

BROMPTON

Brompton Road

④

▶ 17

④ ⑨

▶ 25

Fulham Road

King's Road

BELGRAVIA

③

▶ 33

PIML

CHELSEA

Cheyne Walk

Chelsea Embankment

BATTERSEA   ⑤

⑦